The Gospel of Thomas

Fully Interpreted

The SECRET teachings

hidden beneath the veil

By

H. W. Hodgetts

The Gospel of Thomas Fully Interpreted © 2021 H.W. Hodgetts

ISBN: 9781729450093
Imprint: Independently published

DEDICATION

This book is dedicated to all loving souls who have searched for love, truth and understanding, and to those yet to begin their search.

Introduction

Have you ever looked back through history, from ancient times up until the present day, and wondered how it is that certain people become Kings, Pharaohs and Emperors? How is it that some of these people openly and confidently claimed they were a God, and were indeed worshipped as a God? How can one person hold so much power over so many people? What was the secret of their power?

The answer is of course that they possessed powerful knowledge, and they kept that knowledge secret to preserve their own power and wealth. To preserve that knowledge they hid it in symbols and metaphors, giving the people only a materialistic version. The knowledge that they kept secret was knowledge of the Self, the soul and the mind, and they used it to control people's basic instincts. Those who possessed the secret knowledge became so corrupted by their love of the world that they ended up devoid of empathy, and so being unable to feel what others feel they felt no guilt for causing others suffering and death, and their corruption spread throughout humanity.

Your life is worth nothing to them, but it is to me. So what can be done? I am going to share the secret knowledge with you so that all will be equal and healed.

It is said that if you give a man a fish you feed him for a

day. Teach a man to fish and you feed him for a lifetime.

If we consider that knowledge is food for the soul it can also be said that if you interpret a scripture for a man it will feed his soul for a day. Teach him how to interpret the scriptures for himself and it will feed his soul for a lifetime.

It is my mission to teach you how to interpret the scriptures and discover the secrets hidden beneath the veil that separates the Gospel of the Kingdom within from the gospel of the material world. It is beneath the veil that you will find the most empowering and liberating knowledge in existence and you will discover the answers to all mysteries.

It is said that it is to those who are worthy of the mysteries that the mysteries are given, to others it is not given.

By the time you reach the end of this book, you will have no doubt whether you are worthy of the mysteries or not. If you have understood even a little of what has been written then more will be given to you, because you are worthy.

Love and blessings, William

ltmol@hotmail.co.uk

https:/www.lovethemeaningoflife.com

CONTENTS

Authors Note

The Gospel of Thomas was discovered along with other Gospels, in Nag Hammadi, Egypt, in 1945. These Gospels were rejected by the established church and wrongly judged as heretical. You will come to understand why, when I disclose the correct interpretation of the secret teachings of Jesus, as given in the Gospel of Thomas and translated by Thomas O. Lambdin.

There are 114 logia in the Gospel of Thomas. The term **logia** (Greek: "λόγια", "sayings, utterances, oracles", or singular: "λόγιον", **logion**) is the term applied to collections of sayings credited to Jesus.

Where I have quoted from the New Testament, I have used the King James Version.

I had been a spiritual searcher for most of my life and I have to admit that I was never interested in religious writings. In 2004 I experienced a full and unexpected enlightenment. After that I made it my mission to help people who were suffering spiritually.

In 2012 someone sent me a copy of the Gospel of Thomas and they asked me if I could interpret it. I was very busy at the time but I interpreted all 114 logia in less than a week. I posted it on my website and was then asked if I could publish it in a book which I did.

In the beginning of 2020 I decided to take a look at the interpretations again. I spent much longer on them this time and went into them deeply. The result is this new version which reveals an incredible insight into the mysteries and true teachings of the most loving and enlightened soul to ever walk this earth.

If you like ancient knowledge and secrets your search ends here. Your life is about to be changed in ways you could not imagine.

Love and blessings,

William

The Gospel of Thomas Fully Interpreted

The SECRET teachings behind the veil*

These are the hidden words that the living Jesus spoke and Didymos Judas Thomas wrote them down.

In this opening statement there are two important phrases that need to be fully understood. The first is '**hidden words**', which means that the Logia should not be taken literally, but rather should be considered as esoteric (intended to be revealed only to the initiates of a group.) The secret teachings were presented in this way, because if they had been taught in plain language, then they would soon have incurred the full wrath of what were considered to be, the spiritually blind and dead, and it would not have been possible to preach the Gospel of the Kingdom. You should therefore take into account that many of the words used in the secret teachings are allegorical. (Allegory: a representation of an abstract or spiritual meaning through concrete or material forms; figurative treatment of one subject under the guise of another.) The second phrase to consider is **the living Jesus.** At first glance, you may reason that this refers to Jesus being physically alive at the time when Thomas recorded Jesus' words. However, Thomas was actually referring to Jesus' spiritual state of being.

Logion 1:

He said, "Whoever finds the interpretation of these sayings will not experience death".

Interpretation:

If you were no more than a physical being, then how would it be possible for you to experience anything after your physical body has died? It is plain to see that life and death (as mentioned in the scriptures) are not speaking of physical things. It is a fact that every physical body eventually dies, and once dead it is incapable of experiencing anything.

To *experience* something requires three things; existence, awareness and consciousness. Therefore to experience life or death there must be something that exists after the physical body no longer functions, something that is not of a physical nature, something that is not of this material world.

It is plain to see that these logia and indeed all scriptures, are not teachings things that concern the physical and materialistic world, but rather they are teachings about the spiritual Self, soul and mind. The Self is immortal, why then teach only of temporary things?

Mark 8:36 KJV: *For what shall it profit a man, if he shall gain the whole world, and lose his own soul?*

Whoever finds the interpretations will have found the understanding of truth, and it is this Light of Understanding that gives life to the soul. This Light of Understanding is the <u>Spirit of Truth,</u> also known as the Holy Spirit. Death is only experienced in the absence of this light.

There are three types of soul, each following its chosen path on its life journey.

The first follows the narrow path which is the path of life, which leads to home. It is the right path of righteous desire.

The second is the middle path and is the path of the spiritually diseased, and disabled. These are referred to as sinners who require spiritual healing. It is these that Jesus came to save. They are also referred to as the spiritually *crippled* who require faith. Some are referred to as *the blind* who cannot see the Truth, and some are referred to as *lepers,* who have been misled by false doctrines.

The third is the left path also known as *the ditch.* This is the path of those who are completely materialistic minded, in other words, they have no spiritual understanding; they are the spiritually ***dead*** and *blind.*

They are the dead whose path leads to the oblivion of their souls.

The good news is that those on the middle path can change their path if they wish to.

If you have even a little of the Light of Understanding you will be given more, and what you have cannot be taken away from you.

The key to the scriptures has always been spiritual understanding, and I know it can be difficult at times but do not try to understand or interpret them materialistically.

Come see beneath the veil at what this world has hidden from you, and in seeing you will find yourself.

See also in **John 8:51** KJV: *Verily, verily, I say unto you, If a man keep my saying, he shall never see death.*

Logion 2

Jesus said, "Let him who seeks continue seeking until he finds. When he finds, he will become troubled. When he becomes troubled, he will be astonished, and he will rule over the All."

Interpretation:

What you search for is the Truth and Understanding of yourself, your Soul, and your inner kingdom. When you find these things you will have come to know yourself and you **will become troubled** because you will feel alone and disconnected from the material world, and everything else outside of yourself.

When you become **troubled** you will be **astonished** as you realize that you are the creator and ruler of your inner kingdom and all that there is therein, including your Soul, it is then in your astonishment that you will realize that you are a God and you **will rule over the ALL**, which is everything in your own personal inner spiritual domain.

Logion 3

Jesus said, "If those who lead you say to you, 'See, the kingdom is in the sky,' then the birds of the sky will precede you. If they say to you, 'It is in the sea,' then the fish will precede you. Rather, the kingdom is inside of you, and it is outside of you. When you come to know yourselves, then you will become known, and you will realize that it is you who are the sons of the living father. But if you will not know yourselves, you dwell in poverty and it is you who are that poverty."

Interpretation:

The words *those who lead you* is an obvious reference to the religious authorities, who were teaching a literal and materialistic interpretation of the scriptures.

The kingdom is not *in the sky* or *the sea* of this material world, if it were then the *birds and the fish* would be there before you. *The kingdom* is not of this world, rather *the kingdom is inside* of the Soul *and it is outside* of the Soul. This is because *the kingdom* is the Self's mind, and the Soul is formed from its substance.

When the Souls of the disciples realize what they are, then they *will become known* to each other and they will

8

realize that they are ***the sons of the living father***. The ***father*** being the Self's righteous desire.

But if the Souls ***will not come to know*** themselves then they have nothing of worth, and they are of no worth, because they dwell in the ***poverty*** of ignorance.

See also in **Luke 17:21** KJV: *Neither shall they say, Lo here! or, lo there! for, behold, the kingdom of God is within you.*

Logion 4

Jesus said, "The man old in days will not hesitate to ask a small child seven days old about the place of life, and he will live. For many who are first will become last, and they will become one and the same."

Interpretation:

The man old in days is a reference to the wise soul that is near the end of its life journey.

The *small child seven days old* is a reference to the soul at the beginning of its life journey.

When the wise soul asks the soul at the beginning of its life journey about *the place of life*, he will understand that **the soul is** *the place of life*, and with this understanding his soul will be filled with Life.

The Light of Understanding is the Spirit of Truth, and it is the Spirit that gives life to the Word.

For many souls that took their place in the beginning will take their place also in the end, and both of those souls *will become one and the same*. The end will be the same as the beginning.

See also in **Matthew 18:3** KJV: *And said, Verily I say unto you, Except ye be converted, and become as little children, ye shall not enter into the kingdom of heaven.*

Logion 5

Jesus said, "Recognize what is in your sight, and that which is hidden from you will become plain to you. For there is nothing hidden which will not become manifest."

Interpretation:

That which was *hidden from* the disciples was the kingdom. They could see it but did not recognize it. You too are seeing it even now, but you have not recognized it. The kingdom that should be recognized is of course your mind, your kingdom, your domain.

Every image that you see is in your mind, this is why you can still see things when your physical eyes are closed.

There is seeing and there is perceiving. To perceive is to recognize what you are seeing; to perceive is to understand.

It is when people do not realize that what they are seeing is seen in the mind that the illusion of being in the material world occurs.

Logion 6

His disciples questioned him and said to him, "Do you want us to fast? How shall we pray? Shall we give alms? What diet shall we observe?" Jesus said, "Do not tell lies, and do not do what you hate, for all things are plain in the sight of heaven. For nothing hidden will not become manifest, and nothing covered will remain without being uncovered."

Interpretation:

If you have to ask someone what you should do and how you should behave, then these things are not an expression of what you yourself feels is right. They will simply be done to look good in the eyes of others, and make you feel proud, which would be dishonest and a deception.

If you *tell lies and do what you hate*, you may fool others but you cannot fool yourself, because the Truth will be in your mind. It will trigger your conscience and leave you feeling guilty. What reward do you have then?

Many people *tell lies and do what they hate* because they want to be accepted or loved by others, but even if they succeed they know inside that what they have gained is not deserved, and all it has done is cause harm to the Soul.

Always be honest and true to your feelings, because if you don't you will never know peace, and no-one will ever know the real you.

All things are plain in the sight of heaven (righteous mind).

Logion 7

Jesus said, "Blessed is the lion which becomes man when consumed by man; and cursed is the man whom the lion consumes, and the lion becomes man."

Interpretation:

The *man* represents the soul.

The lion represents desire.

When the soul *consumes* desire his desire becomes righteous.

When desire *consumes* the soul, the soul becomes unrighteous.

Either you rule over desire or desire rulers over you.

If you rule over desire then desire will be *blessed*.

If desire rules over you then you will become *cursed*. There can be only one ruler in your domain/mind.

See also in **1 Peter 5:8** KJV: *Be sober, be vigilant; because your adversary the devil, as a roaring lion, walketh about, seeking whom he may devour.*

Logion 8

And he said, "The man is like a wise fisherman who cast his net into the sea and drew it up from the sea full of small fish. Among them the wise fisherman found a fine large fish. He threw all the small fish back into the sea and chose the large fish without difficulty. Whoever has ears to hear, let him hear."

Interpretation:

In **Matthew 4:19** KJV it is written; *and he saith unto them, Follow me, and I will make you fishers of men.* And so *a wise fisherman* is a reference to a wise disciple.

Preaching to the people is likened to casting a net and attracting a crowd. People caught in the crowd are like fish caught in a *net*.

Souls are likened to *fish*. Souls exist in the mind, and the mind is likened to *the sea.*

The large fish represents a soul that had grown with knowledge and understanding of spiritual things, in other words, a soul that was worthy of the mysteries. *The small fish* represents those not yet ready, or incapable of understanding or perceiving the meanings of the teachings. To be thrown *back* is to be rejected as followers.

16

The wise disciple would choose those who were worthy of the teachings *without difficulty*. *Whoever has the* ability to understand, *let him* understand.

The lesson here is; choose wisely who you choose to teach.

Logion 9

Jesus said, "Now the sower went out, took a handful (of seeds) and scattered them. Some fell on the road; the birds came and gathered them up. Others fell on the rock, did not take root in the soil, and did not produce ears. And others fell on thorns; they choked the seed(s) and worms ate them. And others fell on the good soil and it produced good fruit: it bore sixty per measure and a hundred and twenty per measure."

Interpretation:

The sower is the teacher. *The handful of seeds* represent the teachings of the Gospel of the kingdom.

The seeds represent the Truths in those teachings. The scattering of *the seeds* is the sharing of the teachings with those gathered to hear them.

When hearing the teachings of the kingdom a person will react in one of four ways, and so what happens to the *seeds* of Truth in those teachings is dependent on the person's reaction. Each person will react according to their knowledge, beliefs, level of understanding and desire.

Reaction One

18

The seeds that *fell on the road* are the teachings that were not understood by the one receiving them. *The birds* that *came and gathered them up*, and disposed of them are the thoughts of the one who has an unrighteous heart.

It is this type of person that would judge someone teaching about the kingdom as being foolish.

Reaction Two

The seeds that *fell on the rock*, are the teachings received by the person whose belief in them was temporary and weak. When first heard the teachings made this person feel joyful, but when his belief was tested because of suffering and persecution, the Truth of the teachings of the kingdom died in him without producing any more knowledge of Truth. This is the type of person that has knowledge without faith.

Reaction Three

The seeds that *fell on thorns*, are the teachings rejected by the person whose love of this world and its wealth is too great to accept them. It is the criticisms of his own heart and mind that choke the Truth of the teachings of the kingdom, and so they do not produce more seeds of Truth, and there is no pleasure gained from them.

It is this type of person that loves power and wealth far too much to accept the Truth. In scripture subconscious desires are likened to *worms* that eat the roots of plants.

Reaction Four

The seed that *fell on good soil*, are the seeds of Truth that fall into the open and righteous mind, and then onto the surface of the fertile subconscious mind where they take root. It is then that the seeds of Truth are able to grow and produce a harvest of many more seeds of Truth. Such a person who possesses this type of mind will eventually be filled with Truth, Understanding, and Unconditional Love. To those who have a little more will be given.

See also in **Matthew 13:19-21** KJV: *Hear ye therefore the parable of the sower. When any one heareth the word of the kingdom, and understandeth it not, then cometh the wicked one, and catcheth away that which was sown in his heart. This is he which received seed by the way side. But he that received the seed into stony places, the same is he that heareth the word, and anon with joy receiveth it; Yet hath he not root in himself, but dureth for a while: for when tribulation or persecution ariseth because of the word, by and by he is offended. He also that received seed among the thorns is he that heareth the word; and the care of this world, and the deceitfulness of riches, choke the word, and he becometh unfruitful.* ²³ *But he that received seed into the good ground is he that heareth the word, and understandeth it; which also beareth fruit, and bringeth forth, some an hundredfold, some sixty, some thirty.*

Logion 10

Jesus said, "I have cast fire upon the world, and see, I am guarding it until it blazes."

Interpretation:

It was a burning desire for Truth that Jesus had ignited in the hearts of the people, and he was *guarding it until it* became a passion.

The religious authorities wanted that fire put out, because it was a threat to their power and wealth, and so they began arguing with Jesus in the hope of convincing the people that what Jesus was teaching was wrong. But Jesus countered their accusations with logic and reason, and in this way he was *guarding* the *fire* he had ignited in the hearts of the people.

See also in **Matthew 10:34** KJV: *Think not that I am come to send peace on earth: I came not to send peace, but a sword.*

Logion 11

Jesus said, "This heaven will pass away, and the one above it will pass away. The dead are not alive, and the living will not die. In the days when you consumed what is dead, you made it what is alive. When you come to dwell in the light, what will you do? On the day when you were one you became two. But when you become two, what will you do?"

Interpretation of:

Jesus said, "This heaven will pass away, and the one above it will pass away.

In logion 3 Jesus said *the kingdom is inside of you and it is outside of you*. *The kingdom* is of course a reference to the mind, which is also referred to as *heaven*. Jesus was talking directly to the souls of his disciples, and so when he said *the kingdom is inside of you and it is outside of you* he was saying that heaven/the mind is inside of you and it is outside of you. This is because the soul is formed from and is within the mind.

When Jesus said ***this heaven will pass away*** he was speaking of the disciple's present soul passing away, and when he said ***the one above it will pass away***, he was speaking of the kingdom/mind outside of the soul passing away. This is what happens before the soul is reborn and full enlightenment occurs.

Interpretation of:

The dead are not alive, and the living will not die.

The dead is a reference to the souls who do not possess the Light of Understanding. It is this Light that is the Life of souls. Those who do not possess the Spirit of Understanding have no Life regardless of how much Truth they possess. Therefore the dead are not ***living***. Those who possess the Light of Understanding cannot lose it, therefore they ***will not die***.

Interpretation of:

In the days when you consumed what is dead, you made it what is alive.

That which the disciples ***consumed*** was the Word of Truth and it was with their understanding that they ***made it what is alive***.

The Word without the Spirit of Understanding is like desire without empathy, in other words, it is like an untamed lion. You either rule over desire or it will rule over you.

Interpretation of:

When you come to dwell in the light, what will you do?

When you come to understand *what will you do*?

Jesus said this to his disciples because he knew that when they did come to understand they would have so much to bear.

Interpretation of:

On the day when you were one you became two.

On the day that you possessed the Truth *you were one*, when you possessed the Understanding of Truth *you became two*. In other words, you became the Truth and the Life.

Interpretation of:

But when you become two, what will you do?"

But when you become the Truth and the Life, *what will you do?*

Logion 12

The disciples said to Jesus, "We know that you will depart from us. Who is to be our leader?" Jesus said to them, "Wherever you are, you are to go to James the righteous, for whose sake heaven and earth came into being."

Interpretation:

The disciples were not yet qualified to teach the gospel of the kingdom and they knew that Jesus was going to leave them, so they were concerned about not having a *leader* who would be able to teach them the things they had not yet learned and understood.

James the righteous was the only one besides Jesus who was qualified to teach them because he was full of Truth and Understanding and it was for the sake of Truth and Understanding that *heaven and earth came into being*.

Heaven and earth are of course the conscious and subconscious mind without which, knowledge and understanding could not be discovered.

Logion 13

Jesus said to his disciples, "Compare me to someone and tell me whom I am like." Simon Peter said to him, "You are like a righteous angel." Matthew said to him, "You are like a wise philosopher." Thomas said to him, "Master, my mouth is wholly incapable of saying whom you are like." Jesus said, "I am not your master. Because you have drunk, you have become intoxicated from the bubbling spring which I have measured out." And he took him and withdrew and told him three things. When Thomas returned to his companions, they asked him, "What did Jesus say to you?" Thomas said to them, "If I tell you one of the things which he told me, you will pick up stones and throw them at me; a fire will come out of the stones and burn you up."

Interpretation:

Both **Simon Peter** and **Matthew** perceived only a single aspect of Jesus' character, and so it was easy for each of them to describe who they thought he **was like**. However, Thomas perceived all of the aspects of Jesus' character and so was unable to describe what he was perceiving. In other words, he didn't know anyone who he could compare Jesus to.

26

Thomas had called Jesus **master**, but Jesus had recognized that his student Thomas had learned enough to become a teacher also. This is why Jesus said to Thomas; *I am not your master*.

Knowledge is food for the soul, and so it is said to have been eaten when received. Likewise the spirit is a drink for the soul, and when it is received it is said to have been *drunk*.

Thomas was *intoxicated*, under the influence of the living waters (spirit of understanding) which Jesus had *measured out* to the disciples. It is understanding that gives life.

Jesus *withdrew* from the other disciples so that he could speak to Thomas in private. He then told Thomas *three things*, and what he said was in praise of Thomas and condemnation of the other disciples.

Thomas had sincerely fasted from worldly desires, the other disciples had not. Thomas had prayed in private and with faith, the other disciples had not.

Thomas had given alms without the need for a reward, the others disciples had not.

These *three things* are mentioned in the logion that follows this one.

When Thomas returned to the other disciples they asked him what Jesus had said, but Thomas was worried about how they would react if he told them even one of those things, so he didn't. Thomas knew that they would judge him harshly, in other words, they would ***throw stones*** of judgement at him. They would be words of criticism filled with an unrighteous passion, a strong desire that would consume their goodness.

See in **John 4:14** KJV: *But whosoever drinketh of the water that I shall give him shall never thirst; but the water that I shall give him shall be in him a well of water springing up into everlasting life.*

Logion 14

Jesus said to them, "If you fast, you will give rise to sin for yourselves; and if you pray, you will be condemned; and if you give alms, you will do harm to your spirits. When you go into any land and walk about in the districts, if they receive you, eat what they will set before you, and heal the sick among them. For what goes into your mouth will not defile you, but that which issues from your mouth - it is that which will defile you."

Interpretation:

In the previous logion Thomas had been confronted by the other disciples who wanted to know what Jesus had told him. It was then that Jesus stepped in to take the pressure off Thomas and to give them some advice on their behaviour.

If you *fast* and it is not in your heart to do so, you will leave yourself open to the temptation of doing what you hate, in other words, you will be untrue to yourselves which is a *sin*.

If you *pray you will be condemned* for not having faith.

If you give alms so that you will be praised, *you will do harm to your spirits*.

To *eat what they will set before you*, simply means listen to what they have to say.

To heal the sick means to heal their souls.

The knowledge that you receive from them *will not defile you*, but what you say *it is that which will defile you*. This simply means, be careful what you say.

See also in **Matthew 15:11 KJV:** *Not that which goeth into the mouth defileth a man; but that which cometh out of the mouth, this defileth a man.*

See also in **Matthew 10:8** KJV: *Heal the sick, cleanse the lepers, raise the dead, cast out devils: freely ye have received, freely give.*

Logion 15

Jesus said, "When you see one who was not born of woman, prostrate yourselves on your faces and worship him. That one is your father."

Interpretation:

The *father* of the soul is the Self's righteous desire, and the souls mother is the Self's virgin mind.

The Self and its desire is self-begotten, and so was *not born of woman* i.e. the mind.

Find your righteous heart and you will have found *your father*, and in finding *your father* you will have found yourself.

See also in **Matthew 23:9** KJV: *And call no man your father upon the earth: for one is your Father, which is in heaven.*

Logion 16

Jesus said, "Men think, perhaps, that it is peace which I have come to cast upon the world. They do not know that it is dissension which I have come to cast upon the earth: fire, sword, and war. For there will be five in a house: three will be against two, and two against three, the father against the son, and the son against the father. And they will stand solitary."

Interpretation:

When Jesus spoke of *men* he is referring to the souls of people, and not to their physical bodies which may be either male or female.

When Jesus spoke of *the world* he was referring to the world within. Each soul possesses their own world within, it is a place that we refer to as our mind.

Jesus did not come *to cast* peace on the minds of souls as many had presumed, rather he came to start a spiritual battle within in the mind of souls, a battle between good and evil, and between light and darkness. He came to cast *dissension* on the soul's subconscious mind, (the earth).

There would be *fire* (passion) – *sword* (judgement) – and *war* (conflict).

There will be five in a house. The ***house*** represents the souls personal domain, which as you can see is divided against itself. There will be ***three against two and two against three.***

The **three** that ***are against the two*** represent the righteous ***father***, the faithful ***son***, and the Holy Ghost which is the Spirit of Truth, in other words, the Spirit of Understanding.

The two that are against the three represent the unrighteous father and the son who does not possess the Holy Spirit.

The father that ***is against the son*** represents the unrighteous father against the righteous son.

The ***son*** that ***is against the father*** represent the righteous son against the unrighteous father that is also referred to as *the devil*.

Both the three and the two will stand alone and separate from each other.

See also in **Matthew 10:34-35** KJV: *Think not that I am come to send peace on earth: I came not to send peace, but a sword. For I am come to set a man at variance against his father, and the daughter against her mother, and the daughter in law against her mother in law.*

Logion 17

Jesus said, "I shall give you what no eye has seen and what no ear has heard and what no hand has touched and what has never occurred to the human mind."

Interpretation:

To be able to give someone something, you must first possess it yourself, in other words, Jesus must have *seen* what he wants to show, he must have *heard* what he wants to tell, and he must have *touched* something that he wants others to feel, and something must have occurred to his mind, but not *the human mind*.

That which has not been *seen* has not been imagined.

That which has not been *heard* has not been understood.

That which has not been *touched* has not been felt.

The human mind is a reference to the carnal mind, in other words, the mind of someone who believes that they are no more than a physical being. It is plain that what Jesus wanted to give came from his spiritual mind, and it concerned spiritual things.

Those things are; The Way, the Truth and the Life, which in turn are only seen, heard and felt, by those who are spiritually minded.

See also in **1 Corinthians 2:9** KJV *But as it is written: "Eye hath not seen, nor ear heard, neither have entered into the heart of man the things which God hath prepared for them that love Him."*

Logion 18

The disciples said to Jesus, "Tell us how our end will be." Jesus said, "Have you discovered, then, the beginning, that you look for the end? For where the beginning is, there will the end be. Blessed is he who will take his place in the beginning; he will know the end and will not experience death."

Interpretation:

The disciples knew that the time would come when their physical bodies would cease to function, and they would leave this world. They wanted to know how that *end would be*. In other words, what it would be like.

Jesus reasoned that only a soul that had discovered its first and True Image would be concerned about the end of its journey in this world. Jesus explained to them that their souls would be the same at the end of their journey in this world as they were *in the beginning*.

It is one thing to know what you were in the beginning, and it is another to take that *place in the beginning*. Taking that *place* requires you to lay down all that the world has led you to accept. In other words, you have to take off the garments that have covered your True Image.

Blessed are those that do this, for they ***will know the end and will not experience death,*** which is the complete loss of their True Image of the Self.

Logion 19

Jesus said, "Blessed is he who came into being before he came into being. If you become my disciples and listen to my words, these stones will minister to you. For there are five trees for you in Paradise which remain undisturbed summer and winter and whose leaves do not fall. Whoever becomes acquainted with them will not experience death."

Interpretation of:

Jesus said, "Blessed is he who came into being before he came into being.

The soul first *came into being* in the Self's righteous conscious mind (Heaven) on *the sixth day*. The soul was formed within and from the substance of the Self's righteous and virgin mind.

The second time that the soul *came into being* was when it was retrieved from the subconscious mind and brought back into the conscious mind. The subconscious mind is referred to as *the earth* in scripture, and so the soul was reformed from the substance of the subconscious mind.

So the soul first came into being in Heaven before it came into being from *the dust of the earth*, i.e. the substance of the subconscious mind.

The soul is the Self's image of itself, and in scripture the soul is referred to as *man*.

The first man was made in Heaven on *the sixth day*. The Self rested on *the seventh day*, and on the eighth day the Self remembered its image.

Blessed is the soul that came into being first because it is the Self's true and uncorrupted image. It is that image that the soul strives to restore. This requires the soul's rebirth.

Interpretation of:

If you become my disciples and listen to my words, these stones will minister to you.

In scripture **stones** represent words of judgement. The judgements of Jesus were based on Truth and Understanding, and so by listening to the words of Jesus the needs of the disciples would be taken care of.

Interpretation of:

For there are five trees for you in Paradise which remain undisturbed summer and winter and whose leaves do not fall.

In scripture a book of knowledge is likened to a tree, whose branches represent chapters, and whose leaves represent pages.

Paradise is the enlightened mind. It is the place of the soul's birth and rebirth. It is the place where all Truth is revealed, and it is filled with the Light of Understanding. It is in that place that the peace experienced through true freedom is found, and it is in that place that the bliss of Unconditional Love permeates every part of the soul's whole being. What the soul experiences the Self and the physical body experiences also. *In paradise* there is no fear or need of anything more.

The *five trees in paradise* remain **undisturbed** regardless of what the soul experiences on its life journey.

Summer and winter represent times of strong desire and weak desire. In other words; times of passion and times of apathy. *In paradise* there is neither passion nor apathy. There is no more struggle to fulfil desires because all desires have been fulfilled. It is because of this that emotions are stilled and a perfect state of peaceful bliss is experienced.

The mystery of the five trees

All of the knowledge that you possess has come to you through your five senses. Your physical senses are no more than conduits that pass on information to your spiritual senses. This is why your spiritual senses remain active even when your physical senses are dormant or non-functioning.

The information that your senses receive is entirely dependent on where your attention is focussed, and whatever you focus your attention on will have an effect on what you experience. The stronger you focus your attention, the stronger the effects will be on you, and ultimately your physical body.

The five physical senses transmit information from the material realm to the five spiritual senses which are the receivers. For the purpose of understanding, both sets of senses are likened to each other as an analogy.

Everything that you have experienced in this life journey, has been experienced through your five senses. These are of course the Self's five spiritual senses.

It is important to realize that the five physical senses only gather information from the material world and transfer that information to the Self's spiritual senses. Think of the physical senses as collectors and the spiritual senses as receivers.

Imagine the Self that you refer to as 'I'. Now consider the space that it alone occupies and consider that space as the Self's house. Now imagine the house as having four doors, one door for each of the four spiritual senses. These four doors all lead to the Self and its primary sense of awareness; these are the five senses.

Each spiritual sense gathers a specific category of information, and the Self stores them separately, in other words, each represent a tree of knowledge. Each tree is likened to a book of knowledge. The branches are likened to chapters, and the leaves are likened to pages. Each tree bears its own fruit, which may be bitter or sweet.

There are three things that determine the health, growth and fruit on *the five trees*. These are Understanding, Desire and Truth.

The five trees in paradise are nurtured with Unconditional Love, Truth and Understanding. Their fruit is holy and blissful. Their *leaves do not fall* in times of passion or apathy, because in them is written the Truth.

What are the five spiritual senses?

The five spiritual senses are likened to the five physical senses, but this is only a likeness. Everyone knows what the five physical senses of <u>touch</u>, <u>hearing</u>, <u>sight</u>, <u>smell</u> and <u>taste</u> are, but how are the spiritual senses defined and understood. Let us look at the spiritual senses.

<u>Touch</u> is the primary sense, it is the most important of all the senses; it is the ability to feel and to know. Without this ability there would be no awareness of anything, including the information gathered by the other four senses. Without awareness the Self would remain dormant and even ignorant of its own existence.

<u>Hearing</u> is the ability to interpret information received. When this sense is weak, information received cannot be understood correctly.

<u>Sight</u> is the ability to perceive an image in the mind of information that has been received and interpreted. The intensity of the light in the image is dependent on the validity of what has been interpreted and understood. To see is to understand. It is the light that gives life to the Word.

<u>Smell</u> is the ability to sense the aura surrounding or generated by a person, place or thing. This can be pleasant or disagreeable. What is sensed is the spiritual atmosphere. It is how we sense what is good or evil.

<u>Taste</u> is the ability to sense whether information/knowledge is good or bad for us before we digest it. If this sense is weak then we are prone to believe anything that seems attractive and desirable.

It is the four senses that feed the primary sense of awareness, and if those four senses are weak then they are easily overcome and compromised by unrighteous desire. This is why we should focus our attention on, and question, everything. If we simply accept everything that feels good, our senses will remain weak, and we shall remain in ignorance of the *five trees in paradise*.

Whoever becomes acquainted with them will not experience death, in other words they will experience eternal life, unbroken by reincarnation.

Logion 20

The disciples said to Jesus, "Tell us what the kingdom of heaven is like." He said to them, "It is like a mustard seed. It is the smallest of all seeds. But when it falls on tilled soil, it produces a great plant and becomes a shelter for birds of the sky."

Interpretation:

The first thing to notice is that it says a **great plant** and not a tree.

The kingdom is the Self's mind. **The kingdom of heaven** is the conscious mind that is full of the Light of Understanding. It came into being when the Self first created an image of itself in a small part of the mind. It was in that small part of the mind that **the seed** of faith first came into being.

When that **seed** falls on the **tilled soil** of the subconscious mind it grows like a **great plant**, filling **the kingdom of heaven** with faith, and that faith becomes a **shelter for the birds**, which is a reference to the Self's thoughts.

Both **birds** and *fowl* are references to thoughts, the difference is that *fowl* represent unrighteous thoughts.

The sky is a reference to the lower conscious mind, i.e. the lower part of **heaven** that exists above the subconscious mind. It is likened to this earth's atmosphere.

See also in **Matthew 13:31-32** KJV: *Another parable put he forth unto them, saying, The kingdom of heaven is like to a grain of mustard seed, which a man took, and sowed in his field: Which indeed is the least of all seeds: but when it is grown, it is the greatest among herbs, and becometh a tree, so that the birds of the air come and lodge in the branches thereof.*

Logion 21

Mary said to Jesus, "Whom are your disciples like?" He said, "They are like children who have settled in a field which is not theirs. When the owners of the field come, they will say, 'Let us have back our field.' They (will) undress in their presence in order to let them have back their field and to give it back to them. Therefore I say, if the owner of a house knows that the thief is coming, he will begin his vigil before he comes and will not let him dig through into his house of his domain to carry away his goods. You, then, be on your guard against the world. Arm yourselves with great strength lest the robbers find a way to come to you, for the difficulty which you expect will (surely) materialize. Let there be among you a man of understanding. When the grain ripened, he came quickly with his sickle in his hand and reaped it. Whoever has ears to hear, let him hear."

Interpretation:

The first part of this logion relates to how Jesus is concerned about how his disciples will react when their beliefs are challenged by the temple authorities.

The second part of this logion gives advice on how the disciples should prepare for such an encounter.

The disciples are described as being *like children* because there is still much for them to learn and understand.

The field that they had *settled in* that *was not theirs*, is a reference to the society that they had become accustomed to, a society that had been indoctrinated with materialistic interpretations of the scriptures.

The disciples were of course teaching a spiritual interpretation of the scriptures, which the temple authorities saw as a challenge to their authority over the people. The temple authorities were losing their power over the people along with their wealth and admiration, so they naturally wanted it back. They would do this by challenging and attempting to discredit the disciples and what they believed.

Jesus believed that because of his disciple's lack of knowledge and understanding, they would not be able to defend their beliefs and they would lose their faith. Because of this the disciples would surrender their beliefs and give authority over them to the temple authorities.

In the second part of the logion, Jesus advises his disciples to watch out for those who would challenge their beliefs and not to engage in their arguments. In other words, do not give them the opportunity to dig into their minds and take away the Truth, Understanding, and faith that they have.

To *be on guard against the world* means to; *become a passer-by*. Do not become involved with arguments.

Arm yourself with great strength means; arm yourself with faith.

The difficulty of a challenge to your faith will surely come.

The man of understanding is a reference to the Spirit of Understanding. The angels are the reapers, in other words each of you must possess the Spirit of Understanding.

When the Truth comes to its fruition understanding will come *quickly* and harvest it into your heart.

Whoever is able to receive the Truth let him understand it.

See also in **Matthew 24:43** KJV: *But know this, that if the master of the house had known what hour the thief would come, he would have watched and not allowed his house to be broken into.*

Logion 22

Jesus saw infants being suckled. He said to his disciples, "These infants being suckled are like those who enter the kingdom." They said to him, "Shall we then, as children, enter the kingdom?" Jesus said to them, "When you make the two one, and when you make the inside like the outside and the outside like the inside, and the above like the below, and when you make the male and the female one and the same, so that the male not be male nor the female female; and when you fashion eyes in the place of an eye, and a hand in place of a hand, and a foot in place of a foot, and a likeness in place of a likeness; then will you enter the kingdom."

Interpretation:

In the first part of this logion, Jesus explains to his disciples what they must become *like* if they are to *enter the kingdom*. He then tells them what they must do to become *like little children* to *enter the kingdom*.

When you make the two one. To make the two one the heart must become undivided, meaning that it should not be corrupted with unrighteous desire.

When you make the inside like the outside and the outside like the inside. This part is about making the mind undivided. The soul which is formed from the substance of the mind is referred to as *the inside*, and the mind in which the soul exists and is the soul's domain, is referred to as *the outside*.

And the above like the below. The above is a reference to the head, and the below is a reference to the heart. Usually either the heart rules the head or the head rules the heart. There should be no conflict between them.

And when you make the male and the female one and the same, so that the male not be male nor the female female. This is a reference to the Self's first and True Image of itself in the beginning, also referred to as the Self's soul. This is described in **Genesis 1:27** KJV *So God created man in his own image, in the image of God created he him; male and female created he them.*

When you fashion eyes in the place of an eye. It is with one eye that things are seen, but it is with two eyes that things are perceived, and where there is perception there is understanding. It is prophesied that *they will see but not perceive*. So this part is about perception.

And a hand in place of a hand. This means a healing hand in place of a harming hand.

And a foot in place of a foot. This is about the direction taken in your spiritual life journey. There is the narrow path on which both feet go in the right direction, and there is the wide path when you are not sure where you are going. First one foot takes the lead and then the other.

And a likeness in place of a likeness. This means that you must replace the image that you have of yourself as a physical being, with your first and True Image of your Self as a spiritual being. Then you will come to know your True Self.

Then will you enter the kingdom. When these things are done your soul will enter the kingdom as a little child; your soul will be like it was when first born.

The Self's desire is the Father of the soul, and its Mother is the virgin mind; the birth of the soul is therefore an immaculate conception.

See also in **Matthew 19:14** KJV: *But Jesus said, Suffer little children, and forbid them not, to come unto me: for of such is the kingdom of heaven.*

Logion 23

Jesus said, "I shall choose you, one out of a thousand, and two out of ten thousand, and they shall stand as a single one."

Interpretation:

The one out of a thousand is the one with Love.

Two out of ten thousand are those with Truth and Understanding.

Those who have Love have righteous desire, and so they are the souls that are the children of the Father.

Those that possess the Truth and Understanding are the souls that become the living word.

Together they *shall stand as single one*, in other words the three become one, as in the trinity.

The Father, the Son and the Holy Ghost. These three are therefore the Way (Love), the Truth (the Word) and the Life (the Spirit of Understanding).

The Father becomes the Son, the Son becomes the Father. This is why Jesus said in **John 10:30** KJV; *I and my Father are one.*

Logion 24

His disciples said to him, "Show us the place where you are, since it is necessary for us to seek it." He said to them, "Whoever has ears, let him hear. There is light within a man of light, and he lights up the whole world. If he does not shine, he is darkness."

Interpretation:

It is obvious that the disciples knew where the physical body of Jesus was because they were looking at it, and so didn't need *to seek it*.

It should be realized that all communication between people occurs between their souls. For example, if I speak to you I am not speaking to your physical body but to your soul which animates your body.

It is said that *the eyes are the windows to the soul*, it should also be said that the soul is the doorway to the Self.

What the disciples were seeking and asking to be shown *was the place where* the soul of Jesus was. The disciples had already been taught that the soul exists within and is formed from the substance of mind, in other words, the mind is the world in which the soul exists. Therefore, the disciples wanted to know about the world in which the soul of Jesus was.

Jesus described himself as *the way, the truth and the life,* in other words his soul was formed from *the way*/righteous desire. *The truth*/the Word *and the life*/the Light of Understanding.

When there is the Light of Understanding in the soul, then that light **lights up the whole** mind. If the soul **does not shine**, then the soul does not understand the Truth or what is righteous. It is then that the soul is said to be in the **darkness** of ignorance and is the cause of the **darkness**.

See also in **Matthew 6:22-23** KJV: *The light of the body is the eye: if therefore thine eye be single, thy whole body shall be full of light. But if thine eye be evil, thy whole body shall be full of darkness. If therefore the light that is in thee be darkness, how great is that darkness!*

John 8:12 KJV: *Then spake Jesus again unto them, saying, I am the light of the world: he that followeth me shall not walk in darkness, but shall have the light of life.*

Logion 25

Jesus said, "Love your brother like your soul, guard him like the pupil of your eye."

Interpretation:

It is the way that the most obvious thing is the most difficult to perceive, and what is most obvious here is that there is a difference between you and *your soul*, in other words there is a difference between the Self (that you refer to as 'I') and your soul. The soul is not the Self, the soul is the Self's image of itself, and that image exists outside of the Self in the mind. It is through your image that you interact with all that is outside of you. Therefore the first part of this logion should be read; love other spiritual beings that are like you as you love the image that you have of yourself.

In the second part of this logion, the soul is likened to *the pupil of the eye*, so should be read; *guard your brother's* soul like you guard your own, i.e. help him see and understand clearly.

Logion 26

Jesus said, "You see the mote in your brother's eye, but you do not see the beam in your own eye. When you cast the beam out of your own eye, then you will see clearly to cast the mote from your brother's eye."

Interpretation:

You see the small imperfection *in your brother's* soul, but you do not see the greater imperfection *in your own* soul. *When you cast out* that which is preventing the Light of Understanding from entering your own soul, then you will fully understand how to *cast* out that which is preventing *your brother* from understanding things clearly, otherwise you make yourself a hypocrite.

Those who have less understanding cannot lead those who have more understanding than themselves.

It is easy to see the mistakes that others make, but not so easy to see one's own mistakes. Likewise it is easy to judge others, but not so easy to judge yourself. This is why it was said; *Judge not lest ye be judged.*

See also in **Matthew 7:3-5** KJV: *And why beholdest thou the mote that is in thy brother's eye, but considerest not the beam that is in thine own eye? Or how wilt thou say to thy brother, Let me pull out the mote out of thine eye;*

and, behold, a beam is in thine own eye? Thou hypocrite, first cast out the beam out of thine own eye; and then shalt thou see clearly to cast out the mote out of thy brother's eye.

Logion 27

<Jesus said,> "If you do not fast as regards the world, you will not find the kingdom. If you do not observe the Sabbath as a Sabbath, you will not see the father."

Interpretation:

If you do not completely turn your attention away from this material *world*, and desire nothing that is of it, *you will not find* your spiritual *kingdom* within.

The Sabbath is a time of complete rest, a time of complete detachment, a time where desire is silenced, and the Self's attention is focussed entirely on the Self as it was *in the beginning*. It was then that the Self's state of desire created the Self's first and True Image of itself.

To *see the father* is to see the Self's righteous desire. It is then also that the Self's experiences perfect Love and the soul is reborn, innocent and pure, full of the Light of Understanding.

The end is the same as the beginning.

Logion 28

Jesus said, "I took my place in the midst of the world, and I appeared to them in flesh. I found all of them intoxicated; I found none of them thirsty. And my soul became afflicted for the sons of men, because they are blind in their hearts and do not have sight; for empty they came into the world, and empty too they seek to leave the world. But for the moment they are intoxicated. When they shake off their wine, then they will repent."

Interpretation:

From the Self's perspective it feels like it is in the centre of infinity. There are three places from which the Self feels like it is in the centre of infinity.

The first *place* is where you actually are, it is the place where you first felt your existence and discovered the reality of the Self with the word 'I'. That was the first time where you experienced being in the centre of realty, your reality. This occurred because all of your focus of attention was on yourself and the place in which you alone exist.

The first place was recognized by the Self's sense of feeling.

The second *place* is in the mind, and this illusion is created by the Self's five spiritual senses, especially the sense of sight which is the basis for imagination. In this place the Self can imagine being who they are and where they are. This is where illusions begin and the first place is forgotten. It is not the Self that has moved, rather it is the Self's focus of attention, and it is because of this that the Self creates an alternative Self. This alternative Self is referred to as its soul.

The third *place* is the material world, and this is also an illusion. It is created by the physical body's senses, which create the illusion of the Self being a physical body that is in and of the material realm.

The definition of ego is literally; 'I'.

The definition of alter ego (which represents the soul) is; 'the other I'.

Now we can go back to the logion for it interpretation.

When Jesus *took* his *place in* the *midst of the world,* he was speaking of his soul that was now in possession of a physical body. Those who saw him only saw him as a physical being, in other words he appeared to them in the flesh. This is a problem even today as many people see only the physical bodies of others, they do not see the real person inside.

He *found all of them* overcome by the pleasures of materialism, and *none of them* were *thirsty* for the Spirit of Understanding. They were poisoned by unrighteous desire.

His soul *became afflicted* (troubled) *for the sons of men*, (their souls) because they are blinded by unrighteous desire and they do not understand what they are doing, *for* without a conscience *they came into the world*, and without a conscience *too they seek to leave the world*.

But for the moment they are overcome by materialistic desires. *When they shake of their* love of the world, *then they will repent*.

Logion 29

Jesus said, "If the flesh came into being because of spirit, it is a wonder. But if spirit came into being because of the body, it is a wonder of wonders. Indeed, I am amazed at how this great wealth has made its home in this poverty."

Interpretation:

If the reason for *the flesh* coming *into being was because of the spirit, it is a wonder.*

If the reason for *the spirit* coming *into being was* the body, *it is a wonder of wonders*.

The question is; what came into being first, *the flesh* that forms the physical body, or the spiritual attributes of awareness, desire and will?

For a bunch of biological cells to form and then crawl out of a swamp, it would require awareness of its environment, and the desire to leave that environment. It would also mean that these attributes would have to form through a massive amount of chance events. Imagine the amount of cells this would require, and the space that it would take up. Then consider the size of an ant's brain. If you watch an ant, or even a flea, how can you say that it doesn't have awareness, desire and will?

Without awareness, desire and will, flesh and the body it forms would remain inanimate, and without a mind it would remain unconscious.

The Self is a spiritual being, it animates the physical body, so it is the *spirit* that must exist before the requirement of a physical body.

It is amazing how the *spirit* has ***made its home*** in that which is a material thing. *Poverty* here is the lack of life, which is the lack of understanding. The physical body is not even aware of its own existence, but the Self is.

Logion 30

Jesus said, "Where there are three gods, they are gods. Where there are two or one, I am with him."

Interpretation:

The first thing to understand is that **gods** are rulers, and they rule according to their own desire.

First of all notice that is says **three gods** it doesn't say three or more gods; it is three only.

Secondly, notice that the word **gods** is spelt with a lower case **g**. There is a difference between **God** and **god**.

One of the greatest deceptions of the false teachers, was to hide the fact that the word **God** actually represents the Self that you refer to as 'I'. This knowledge was the first key to understanding the scriptures, and by hiding it the Pharisees and scribes were able to teach a false version of the Old Testament. This is why a New Testament was needed; a spiritual one and not a materialistic one.

The second deception was to hide the fact that a **god** represents the Self's image i.e. the Self's soul, also referred to as the Self's alter ego.

The Latin definition of 'I' is ego.

The Latin definition of 'alter ego' is 'the other I'.

The greatest deception of all was to give a materialistic interpretation of the scriptures in place of a spiritual one, this had the effect of hiding all of the keys and the way to the kingdom.

The *three gods* are three versions of the soul, in other words, the three images that the Self may have of itself, and they are:

The Self's first and True Image created in heaven, i.e. the righteous conscious mind.

The second image retrieved from the earth, i.e. subconscious mind (Adam).

The third is the corrupted image of the second image (Satan).

Now for the part of this logion that says; *where there are two or one, I am with him.*

The *two* represent the first and True Image created in heaven, and the uncorrupted image retrieved from the subconscious mind, as a perfect memory of the first image.

It was inevitable that while on a life journey animating a physical body that the Self would be subjected to temptation and would make errors, but this was after all, a journey of learning. The result of pursuing pleasure without wisdom was that the Self's desire, i.e. its heart became divided, and sought pleasure from what was good and from what was evil. Whichever side the Self chose would have an effect on the Self's image/soul.

It is when the Self regains its original image and is in harmony with the Self's righteous desire that the two images *become one* and the same.

The Self's desire is the father/creator of the Self's image, and when the heart is divided so also is the Self's image.

It is the Self's desire that determines which side of its image/soul will have dominion over the ALL, in other words, the Self's soul will either rule as a Christ or a Satan.

So *where there are three gods* there is conflict between good and evil. *Where there are two or one* there is peace.

See also **1 John 3:2** KJV: *Beloved, now are we the sons of God, and it doth not yet appear what we shall be: but we know that, when he shall appear, we shall be like him; for we shall see him as he is.*

Logion 31

Jesus said, "No prophet is accepted in his own village; no physician heals those who know him."

Interpretation:

No-one who has known you as an ordinary person, will accept you as being any different to what they have known.

No-one is born a *prophet*, it is a skill that has to be acquired through learning and understanding.

It is said that familiarity breeds contempt and that is exactly what happens when you try to teach people who knew you before you changed. They will reject what you say because they have no faith in you, especially when you challenge their beliefs.

It is the same for a *physician*, because to receive healing one must first have faith in the healer.

This logion is of course about healing the souls of people.

See also in **Luke 4:24** *And he said, Verily I say unto you, No prophet is accepted in his own country.*

Logion 32

Jesus said, "A city being built on a high mountain and fortified cannot fall, nor can it be hidden."

Interpretation:

The *city being built* is a spiritual one, and its name is New Jerusalem. It is a place where the souls of the disciples are gathered together as a single tribe.

The houses that form the city and in which each soul of the disciples dwell, are built from knowledge of Truth.

The *high mountain* on which the *city* is *being built*, is the Spirit of Understanding. It is fortified by faith and so *cannot fall, nor can it be hidden* because of the Light of Understanding.

There are seven spirits and these are likened to mountains, the first and most important and the one mentioned here, is the Spirit of Understanding.

The roots of the *mountain* are in and of the earth, which spiritually is the subconscious mind, and each *mountain* reaches *high* up into the conscious mind, and so it is the conscious mind that sits upon the mountain i.e. seven spirits.

Logion 33

Jesus said, "Preach from your housetops that which you will hear in your ear. For no one lights a lamp and puts it under a bushel, nor does he put it in a hidden place, but rather he sets it on a lampstand so that everyone who enters and leaves will see its light."

Interpretation:

Share with others the things that I teach you, do it openly and with confidence. Let them see the Light of your new Understanding. Do not be afraid to share what you have been given.

That which the disciples *heard in* their *ears* was the true interpretation of Jesus' words, and in hearing his words they understood what was really being said.

Jesus gave the disciples the secret knowledge, but it was the disciples who gave life to that knowledge with their Spirit of Understanding, which is the Light of Life.

No-one who understands the Truth puts it in a place where that *light* will go out, nor do they keep it *hidden* from others, but rather they put it in the open in a place of faith, and they show it to others with confidence to *light* their way in the darkness.

See also in **Matthew 5:15** KJV: *Neither do men light a candle and put it under a bushel, but on a candlestick, and it giveth light unto all that are in the house.*

Logion 34

Jesus said, "If a blind man leads a blind man, they will both fall into a pit."

Interpretation:

It is not enough to have knowledge, one must also have understanding. If a man without understanding leads a man without understanding, *they will both fall into a pit* of ignorance and *death*.

To be spiritually *blind* is to be unable to see the Light of Understanding.

See also in **Matthew 15:14** KJV: *Let them alone: they be blind leaders of the blind. And if the blind lead the blind, both shall fall into the ditch.*

Logion 35

Jesus said, "It is not possible for anyone to enter the house of a strong man and take it by force unless he binds his hands; then he will (be able to) ransack his house."

Interpretation:

The house represents the mind. The strength of a man is determined by his confidence in his beliefs. You cannot make a man change his beliefs and accept yours unless you first destroy that confidence. If you can use logic to show a man that his beliefs are in error, then you can prevent him from defending them and you can challenge all of his beliefs. Think of how Jesus dealt with those who opposed him. He used their own doctrines and beliefs against them and in doing so made their wisdom look foolish.

See also **Matthew 12:29** KJV: *Or else how can one enter into a strong man's house, and spoil his goods, except he first bind the strong man? And then he will spoil his house.*

Note: It should also be realized that even today, the houses of many loving souls are being ransacked by materialists, because they do not have the Truth or the wisdom to defend their Love.

Logion 36

Jesus said, "Do not be concerned from morning until evening and from evening until morning about what you will wear."

Interpretation:

The clothes that are being referred to here are not the type used to cover the physical body, but rather they are a reference to the spiritual clothes that cover the soul.

Consider that a physical baby is born without clothes, and likewise a soul is born without spiritual clothes.

Just as material clothes are used to hide the image of the physical body, so also are spiritual clothes used to hide the image of the soul.

It is what is hidden beneath the clothes that matters, and if you care to look, you will find the most unrighteous of people dressed in the most expensive of clothes, and the most righteous dressed in rags or cheap common clothing.

It is said that '*you must become like little children*', because little children have no shame, guilt or vanity. They do not hide their feelings, they are innocent and do not care about what others think, they are not concerned about what they do not know or understand. They are new to the world, uncorrupted and free spirited. It is only later that the world takes away all that they had and compels them to put on clothes to hide their body and soul.

Do not be concerned about what you will wear, be concerned about your soul, about the Truth of what you are, and about what is good and right. These are the things you began your journey with.

See also in **Matthew 6:28-30** KJV: *And why take ye thought for raiment? Consider the lilies of the field, how they grow; they toil not, neither do they spin: And yet I say unto you, That even Solomon in all his glory was not arrayed like one of these. Wherefore, if God so clothe the grass of the field, which to day is, and to morrow is cast into the oven, shall he not much more clothe you, O ye of little faith?*

Logion 37

His disciples said, "When will you become revealed to us and when shall we see you?" Jesus said, "When you disrobe without being ashamed and take up your garments and place them under your feet like little children and tread on them, then will you see the son of the living one, and you will not be afraid"

Interpretation:

The first part of this logion appears to be a single question that is repeated in a different way. It will be realized however that there are actually two separate questions being asked by the disciples. The two questions may also appear strange considering that Jesus is standing there in their company, so it should be obvious that the disciples are not referring to something physical, but rather to something spiritual that is hidden within.

Jesus was a spiritual being as we all are, but being distracted by the world, people become blind to the reality of their true nature, and so people only see the physical appearance of others and of themselves, they do not see that which is animating the physical body. It is when *you come to know yourself* that you see the souls of others, the real person inside.

Every soul at the beginning had the same image as each other, an uncorrupted image of perfect light, full of innocence and beauty. It was the first and True Image of the Self as a God.

The questions are really; when will we become as you? And when will we see you as a spiritual being?

The second part of this logion Jesus tells his disciples what they must do to also overcome the world and become *like little children* once more.

To *disrobe* is to *take off the garments* of judgement; both the judgements that others who are ignorant have placed on you, and those judgements that you have placed on yourself, and this must be done *without being ashamed*.

When *little children* tread on their *garments* it means that those garments mean nothing to them, they are not accepted as their belongings. Ignorance belongs to only to the ignorant.

The living one is the Self that is filled with Love, Truth and the Light of Understanding, which is the Life, and its soul is its True Image; its *son*. When you see your True Image, the one that you had in the beginning, *you will not be afraid*.

See also in **Matthew 18:3** KJV: *And said, Verily I say unto you, Except ye be converted, and become as little children, ye shall not enter into the kingdom of heaven.*

Logion 38

Jesus said, "Many times have you desired to hear these words which I am saying to you, and you have no one else to hear them from. There will be days when you will look for me and will not find me."

Interpretation:

The **words** that the disciples had **desired to hear many times** and what Jesus was saying to them, were of course the secret teachings that had been hidden in the scriptures from those who were spiritually blind and carnal minded.

Those who were teaching the scriptures only gave the people a literal interpretation, thereby convincing them that the scriptures were all about the material world, just as the church does today. Jesus was the only one teaching the spiritual interpretation of the scriptures, which were about the world within, in other words, the Gospel of the Kingdom. There was **no-one else** that the disciples could receive these teachings from other than Jesus.

The disciples were not yet capable of seeing the real Jesus inside, at this point they only saw him as a physical being. Therefore these are **the days** when they could **not find** nor see the soul of Jesus, but eventually they would.

See also in **John 7:34** KJV: *Ye shall seek me, and shall not find me: and where I am, thither ye cannot come.*

Logion 39

Jesus said, "The Pharisees and the scribes have taken the keys of knowledge (gnosis) and hidden them. They themselves have not entered, nor have they allowed to enter those who wish to. You, however, be as wise as serpents and as innocent as doves."

Interpretation:

The Pharisees and scribes were those who preserved the Word, but hid its spiritual meanings, which were the keys of understanding the Word.

The Word without the Spirit of Understanding is a dead letter. What good is any knowledge without understanding?

The Pharisees and scribes did not enter the kingdom within because it would have meant they would have had to give up their power and wealth. They did not give the people the spiritual interpretations of the scriptures, thereby not allowing them to enter the kingdom, because the people would then be free, and they would then see the Pharisees and scribes as false teachers.

Knowledge is the door; Understanding is the key.

To **be as wise as serpents and as innocent as doves** means; be as wise as the false teachers and avoid conflict by being peaceful. Jesus referred to the false teachers as a *nest of vipers*, in other words, they will attack you if you challenge them.

See also in **Luke 11:52 KJV:** *Woe unto you, lawyers! for ye have taken away the key of knowledge: ye entered not in yourselves, and them that were entering in ye hindered.*

Logion 40

Jesus said, "A grapevine has been planted outside of the father, but being unsound, it will be pulled up by its roots and destroyed."

Interpretation:

Think of the Gospel of the kingdom as *a grapevine* that grows in the mind, its roots reach down into the subconscious mind.

It can be seen that there are two vines in this logion, one of them has been planted outside of the Self's righteous desire, and therefore it is not of Truth, i.e. it is not righteous.

The true vine contains the knowledge that the Self is a spiritual being, whereas the grapevine planted *outside of* righteous desire contains the knowledge that the Self is a physical being, it is that knowledge that is unsound; it is like a house built on sand.

See also in **John 15:1** KJV: *I am the true vine, and my Father is the husbandman.*

Logion 41

Jesus said, "Whoever has something in his hand will receive more, and whoever has nothing will be deprived of even the little he has."

Interpretation:

Whoever has some light of the Spirit of Understanding *in his hand will receive more*, and he will be able to interpret the scriptures spiritually, thereby revealing their hidden meanings, in other words his understanding and interpretation of them will be correct.

And whoever has no light of the Spirit of Understanding *will be deprived of even the little* literal understanding that *he has*, because his interpretations are incorrect.

It is a spiritual understanding that gives life to the scriptures.

The Truth will set you free, but only if you understand it spiritually.

See also in **Matthew 25:29** KJV: *For unto every one that hath shall be given, and he shall have abundance: but from him that hath not shall be taken away even that which he hath.*

Logion 42

Jesus said, "Become passers-by."

Interpretation:

Simply put this means; choose peace, peace before pleasure. Step out of the game of life, which has become the pursuit and experience of pleasure, even to the cost of your soul. Do not make attachments because at both ends of the attachment, there is a loss of freedom.

Step out of the game of life being played in this world, because no-one wins in the end.

Sometimes you have to give in to win. The more that you want something, the more it will resist you. It is when you are content with what you have that good things come to you.

Peace is the place where Unconditional Love resides, there is no greater pleasure.

Logion 43

His disciples said to him, "Who are you that you should say these things to us?" <Jesus said to them,> "You do not realize who I am from what I say to you, but you have become like the Jews, for they either love the tree and hate its fruit (or) love the fruit and hate the tree."

Interpretation:

It is plain to see that the disciples were questioning the authority of Jesus to teach them. This was because they either had difficulty accepting his teachings, or difficulty in abiding by them.

They had not yet realized that Jesus was the Way, the Truth and the Life, a perfected soul full of Unconditional Love, Truth and Understanding. They had not even realized that he was a spiritual being, or that it was a soul that was speaking to them; a soul that had found peace in a world of conflict.

They had become like those following a materialistic interpretation of the Judaic scriptures.

For they either loved the Word but hated the reward of abiding by it.

Or they loved the reward but hated the Word.

There were those who were fascinated by the teachings but hated having to suffer by following their commandments, and there were those like the temple authorities, who loved the power and wealth they gained from teaching the scriptures, but they themselves hated the scriptures because if the Truth of them was known by others, it would expose them as false teachers, and they would lose their power, wealth and standing in the community.

Pleasurable things are easily accepted, but when the pleasure ends there is only rejection.

It is Understanding that brings perfect peace.

Logion 44

Jesus said, "Whoever blasphemes against the father will be forgiven, and whoever blasphemes against the son will be forgiven, but whoever blasphemes against the Holy Spirit will not be forgiven either on earth or in heaven."

Interpretation:

The father is a reference to the Self's desire. It is the Self's desire that precedes all of the Self's actions, including the acts of creation and control.

Everything that exists in the Self's spiritual domain (mind) is created by the Self's desire, and these things are created according to the Self's knowledge and understanding. In the beginning the Self knew and understood only what was good and right. It was only when knowledge of what was **not** good and right was discovered that the Self's desire was divided and the Self lost its way.

The meaning of life is to pursue and experience pleasure, and in the beginning that pleasure was righteous and caused no harm, but on the discovery of knowledge that was a corruption of Truth, the Self now had two opposing ways for its desire to pursue and experience pleasure.

'The purpose of a life journey is to learn how to pursue and experience pleasure without causing harm to the Self's soul, or to the souls of others'. William

We are sometimes influenced by unrighteous desire or by others, to create things in the mind that cause conflict and offence, between our divided desire according to which side is dominant, and according to our understanding or ignorance. This is when the Self's soul begins to **blaspheme against** its **father**, i.e. desire. This **will be forgiven** due to lack of Understanding.

The son is a reference to the Self's soul created by the Self's desire. The soul is an image of the Self created in the mind by the Self's desire. In the beginning that image was of Love, Truth and Understanding, and because the Self's desire had not yet been divided, the soul represented the Self's True Image. This image was created in the first seven days of the Self's life journey, (as I have explained in my book, Genesis the Beginning). **The father** of the Self's soul is the Self's desire, and its mother is the Self's righteous and uncorrupted mind.

It is through the soul that the Self and its desire interacts with the spiritual and the material realms.

When the Self's desire becomes divided because of the knowledge of good and evil, the soul becomes divided also. This means there are two fathers and two sons, one of righteous desire and one of unrighteous desire. Think of this as having one soul with two opposing personalities. When the soul is divided in this way, each side will *blaspheme* against the other soul's father, but they *will be forgiven* because of the lack of Understanding.

It was never the Self that was in danger of eternal damnation, it was only ever the unrighteous and ignorant soul. The Self and its True Image are immortal, and where a soul is discarded due to its corruption, the Self will begin a new life journey with a soul that is its True Image.

You should now understand why Jesus said to the Pharisees: '*Your father is the devil*', which is a reference to their evil heart.

The Holy Spirit is the Spirit of Truth, and the Spirit of Truth is the Understanding of Truth. It is the light that gives life to the Word, without which the Word is a *dead letter*. To receive *the Holy Spirit* is to receive enlightenment in the soul, and this light lights up the whole mind. Truth without the Light of Understanding leaves the soul and the mind in the darkness of ignorance.

Whoever blasphemes against the Holy Spirit also blasphemes against the Self and it's True Image. How then can their soul be forgiven by the Self?

If you hate yourself, if you feel you are not worth anything and you are not worthy of Love, it is because you do not know your True Self anymore. You must come to know yourself, and that your True Image was created by Love in the Light of Understanding, which is *the Holy Spirit*.

The Holy Spirit is also known as the *comforter*, because it is true understanding that brings inner peace; a peace that cannot be taken away.

Love yourself according to the Love you have for others.

Love gave you an image of yourself, the world replaced it with a false one. You are neither in this world nor of it.

Your soul is your inner child; save it while you are able.

See also in **Matthew 12:31-32** KJV: *Wherefore I say unto you, All manner of sin and blasphemy shall be forgiven unto men: but the blasphemy against the Holy Ghost shall not be forgiven unto men.*

Logion 45

Jesus said, "Grapes are not harvested from thorns, nor are figs gathered from thistles, for they do not produce fruit. A good man brings forth good from his storehouse; an evil man brings forth evil things from his evil storehouse, which is in his heart, and says evil things. For out of the abundance of the heart he brings forth evil things."

Interpretation:

Grapes are *harvested* from a grapevine. In John 15:1 KJV Jesus says; '*I am the true vine, and my Father is the husbandman*'. *Father* is a reference to the Self's righteous heart, and the soul of Jesus is the Son, i.e. the True Image of the Father, and through Jesus the Father spread the Gospel of the Kingdom, and so Jesus became like a vine, his branches were his disciples who produced the fruit of the gospel, and when the disciples gave the fruit to others, the seeds of Truth were planted within those souls also.

The fruit of the kingdom is *not harvested* from those whose hearts are *evil* and believe in a false doctrine, for they produce only the hurtful *thorns* of hateful criticism and condemnation.

Figs which represent hidden knowledge are not ***gathered from thistles***, which represent the materialistic interpretations of the souls who are referred to as the *blind and the dead*, and whose *father is the devil*, which is a reference to the evil heart.

So the teaching here is; only teach the Gospel of the Kingdom to those who have good hearts and therefore able to receive it. Do not waste your time teaching those whose hearts are evil and whose only love is for themselves and this world.

You too be careful who you share the gospel with for some will not understand, and some will hate you for speaking the Truth, and for condemning this world that they love even more than other souls.

See also in **Matthew 7:16-18** KJV: *Ye shall know them by their fruits. Do men gather grapes of thorns, or figs of thistles? Even so every good tree bringeth forth good fruit; but a corrupt tree bringeth forth evil fruit. A good tree cannot bring forth evil fruit, neither can a corrupt tree bring forth good fruit.*

Logion 46

Jesus said, "Among those born of women, from Adam until John the Baptist, there is no one so superior to John the Baptist that his eyes should not be lowered (before him). Yet I have said, whichever one of you comes to be a child will be acquainted with the kingdom and will become superior to John."

Interpretation:

If you interpret this logion literally then you are left with the problem that Adam did not have a physical mother. The key to understanding is as follows:

In scripture the spiritual interpretation of **woman** is mind.

Here the word *women* is spelled without capitals, and so it refers to the subconscious mind, also referred to as *the earth*.

Adam (the first man) was created from the *dust of the earth*, which means that he was a memory of the Self's first image, which had been created in heaven. You should realize that what is being spoken of in this logion are souls, not physical beings.

So every soul born of the Self's subconscious mind, from *Adam until John the Baptist* was so *superior* that anyone seeing *John the Baptist* should *lower their eyes* in respect of his superiority.

John was seen as *superior* because he possessed the Truth, i.e. the Word and the ability to baptize others unto repentance with it.

To *become a child* means that as a soul you must sacrifice what the world has led you to believe about yourself, and in coming to know yourself, be reborn as the image of righteous desire, and of the righteous mind.

Then you will take off the garments that those of this world had given you to wear, and you will stand on them absent of shame. That is how you return to the *Kingdom* of Heaven from where you first came. You will of course still be in control of your physical body through which you will interact with this world, until that body no longer functions. It is not a physical death that is experienced, rather it is a spiritual death and rebirth of your soul. You will *become superior to John the Baptist* because you will possess not only the Word, but also the Holy Spirit.

See also in **Matthew 11:11** KJV: *Verily I say unto you, Among them that are born of women there hath not risen a greater than John the Baptist: notwithstanding he that is least in the kingdom of heaven is greater than he.*

Logion 47

Jesus said, "It is impossible for a man to mount two horses or to stretch two bows. And it is impossible for a servant to serve two masters; otherwise, he will honor the one and treat the other contemptuously. No man drinks old wine and immediately desires to drink new wine. And new wine is not put into old wineskins, lest they burst; nor is old wine put into a new wineskin, lest it spoil it. An old patch is not sewn onto a new garment, because a tear would result."

Interpretation:

In scripture a desire is likened to a *horse*, this is because desire carries you to where you want to go. Without desire you would go nowhere.

When the heart is divided it means you have a choice of which horse to ride, in other words, you have a choice between righteous desire and unrighteous desire.

It is impossible for the soul *to mount two horses* because they go in different directions.

Where there are two opposing desires it is only possible to choose one or the other at a time.

Likewise it is impossible to be passionate about both righteous desire and unrighteous desire at the same time, because this would weaken the soul's willpower.

Changing *horses* often means you will not reach the kingdom of heaven.

When the heart is divided it is impossible for the soul to serve both sides of it. Whichever side he honours, he with treat the other contemptuously.

Before Jesus began teaching a New Testament, the scriptures had been interpreted literally, that is to say the Word was taught *without the Spirit*.

Even as it was, those who received the literal interpretations were filled with much pleasure, this was because they were led to believe the Word alone was their way to salvation and eternal life, but it was not.

The Word without the Spirit is a *dead letter*, and so those who had only received and accepted the literal word, were referred to as **the dead** and **the blind**; blind because they had no Light of Understanding in them.

Then Jesus came with a New Testament. He was a witness not only of the Word, but also the Spirit of the Word. He found them all **intoxicated** with wine of the Word without the Spirit, and some of them immediately desired **to drink the new wine** of the New Testament.

Wine is a reference to the pleasure of the knowledge within.

Wineskin is a reference to the soul.

The New Testament of the Word and the Spirit is not given to those whose faith is in the literal teachings of the Word alone, because they will be unable to contain it and will reject it, lest they lose everything and become empty, nor is the pleasure of the Word alone given to new students, lest it *spoil* their soul.

An old patch is not sewn onto a new garment. This is because the New Testament is stronger than the Old Testament. In other words the Word and the Spirit is stronger than the Word alone.

See also in **Matthew 9:17 KJV:** *Neither do men put new wine into old bottles: else the bottles break, and the wine runneth out, and the bottles perish: but they put new wine into new bottles, and both are preserved.*

Logion 48

Jesus said, "If two make peace with each other in this one house, they will say to the mountain, 'Move Away,' and it will move away."

Interpretation:

If the Father and the Son *make peace* in the Self's uncorrupted mind, *they will say to the mountain* of ignorance, *'Move Away' and it will move away*.

Ignorance is likened to a *mountain* that is between the Father and the Son. *The mountain* is not only an obstacle it also blocks the light and casts a shadow, and that shadow is referred to as *the shadow of death*.

It is this mountain that separates the Self's desire from the souls desire, thereby limiting the power of both. When the two desires are as one then nothing can resist its will.

The mind is divided into many houses, each according to the soul's personality. Some belong to the righteous heart, some belong to the unrighteous heart, and some belong to neither. Those that will stand firm are those built with Love on the foundations of Truth and filled with the Light of Understanding.

Many souls have sought power for themselves, but the ultimate power has always been the Self's righteous desire; it is the power of Love. It is unconditional, pure and eternal. If you become one with it you too will inherit its power.

The Father becomes the Son, the Son becomes the Father.

See also in **Matthew 21:21** KJV *Jesus answered and said unto them, Verily I say unto you, If ye have faith, and doubt not, ye shall not only do this which is done to the fig tree, but also if ye shall say unto this mountain, Be thou removed, and be thou cast into the sea; it shall be done.*

Logion 49

Jesus said, "Blessed are the solitary and elect, for you will find the kingdom. For you are from it, and to it you will return."

Interpretation:

The solitary are souls that are undivided by righteous and unrighteous desire, in other words, they do not have a split personality. They are referred to as *the elect* because they have been chosen to represent the Self's righteous desire and its True Image.

You will find *the kingdom* of heaven (the Self's righteous mind) because you *are from it, and to it you will return*, in other words, your soul will return home to be with its Creator; your father, your Self's righteous desire.

If you have looked at this world and recognized the evil and ignorance of others, and you have felt sorrow and loneliness, then it is you who are the *solitary and elect*, it is you who are from the light and to the light you will return. Your nature will have driven you to search for Love, Truth, Understanding, and for knowledge of the Self. You are not alone and you were always loved. Dare to be who you are, hold your head up and come out of the shadows. Your place is in the light.

Logion 50

Jesus said, "If they say to you, 'Where did you come from?' say to them, 'we came from the light, the place where the light came into being on its own accord and established itself and became manifest through their image.' If they say to you, 'is it you?' say, 'We are its children, we are the elect of the living father.' If they ask you, 'What is the sign of your father in you?' say to them, 'It is movement and repose.'"

Interpretation of: Jesus said, "If they say to you, 'Where did you come from?'

If you perceive yourself as no more than a physical being, then your answer to the question; *'Where did you come from?'* will either be from your physical parents or from a certain place in this world. But if you have realized that you are a soul and therefore a spiritual being, then your answer should be as Jesus explains.

Interpretation of: say to them, 'we came from the light the place where the light came into being on its own accord and established itself and became manifest through their image.'

The light is the Spirit of Truth, and the Truth is the Word. Now consider the following scriptures:

In the beginning was the word and the word was with God, and the word was God. **John 1:1** KJV. The real meaning of this is as follows:

In the beginning was the Truth and the Truth was with the Self and the Truth was the Self; that Truth was of course; **I AM**.

In the beginning there was no light in the Self's virgin mind, and so although the Self was aware of its existence, it had no understanding of what it was. At this point it was a case of; I AM, but what AM I?

In Genesis on the first day (and after becoming Self-aware), the Self's desire moved it to seek understanding of the Truth it had felt within. '*Let there be light*, means; let there be understanding. This was a desire; a desire that the Self did not have the knowledge to fulfil. There then appeared an image in the virgin mind, an image formed of *light*, and it *came into being* and had made itself permanent *on its own accord*.

The light of the image *became manifest* through the image of the Self's Truth and its righteous desire. The Self now knew and understood all that it was, I AM now became, I AM that I AM, in other words; I know myself.

Interpretation of: If they say to you, 'is it you?' say, 'We are its children, we are the elect of the living father.'

Souls are spiritual entities and just like children, they are not self-created, likewise each child has a father and a mother.

In the spiritual realm *the father* of the soul's creation is righteous desire, and the mother is the righteous mind. It is *the father* that plants the seed of the soul, and it is the mother that gives it life. Every soul was created from Love, Truth and Understanding, and so was perfect in the beginning.

When the disciples say; *We are its children*, they are saying; we are the True Image of the Self. When they say; *we are the elect of the living father*, they are saying; we are the chosen of *the living father*.

The father is referred to as *living*, because the Self's desire also has the Light of Understanding which is the Life.

The Light of Understanding is of course the Spirit of Truth, also referred to as the Holy Spirit.

Jesus was a soul who referred to himself as *the way the truth and the life*, which is righteous desire (Love), Truth (the Word) and the Spirit of Truth, (the Life).

Interpretation of: If they ask you, 'What is the sign of your father in you?' say to them, 'It is movement and repose.'"

The sign of the father is of course righteous desire and peace; peace because desire has been fulfilled. They had sought and they had found. Desire causes *movement*, and the fulfilment of desire results in rest (*repose*).

Logion 51

His disciples said to him, "When will the repose of the dead come about, and when will the new world come?" He said to them, "What you look forward to has already come, but you do not recognize it."

Interpretation:

There are those who have studied and learned every word of the scriptures, but without the spiritual understanding of them, they are only able to interpret those scriptures literally. This leads them to believe that the scriptures speak only of the things of this material realm. It is because of this that they believe that they are in and of this world. They believe that they are physical beings, and that heaven is a place in this material realm/universe. People with such beliefs are regarded as the ignorant and dead; ignorant because they do not understand the Truth or the Holy Spirit or the Light of Understanding.

The disciples had looked *forward to* receiving the spirit, and through understanding the receiving of peace. They were also waiting for *the new world* (kingdom) to *come*.

They had already received the Light of Understanding from Jesus, and their inner world had already changed, but they had not *recognized* these things.

That which is most obvious is usually the most difficult to *recognize*.

Logion 52

His disciples said to him, "Twenty-four prophets spoke in Israel, and all of them spoke in you." He said to them, "You have omitted the one living in your presence and have spoken (only) of the dead."

Interpretation:

The **Twenty-four prophets** are the *Twenty-four elders* who all spoke in the name of Truth, but they did not possess the Spirit of Truth, which is the light of spiritual understanding, because of this they were regarded as **dead**.

Jesus possessed the Word and the Spirit, and so he was **the one living**.

It is written that *the word without the spirit is a dead letter*.

The letter kills, the spirit gives life. **2 Corinthians 3:6 KJV**.

Knowledge without understanding results in ignorance. When that knowledge is of spiritual things and is absent of understanding, then it is the Self's soul that is in peril.

Logion 53

His disciples said to him, "Is circumcision beneficial or not?" He said to them, "If it were beneficial, their father would beget them already circumcised from their mother. Rather, the true circumcision in spirit has become completely profitable."

Interpretation:

The message here is that physical circumcision is not natural, *if it were* they would be born *already circumcised*. It is actually MGM, male genital mutilation. Physical circumcision may be beneficial physically, but it is not beneficial spiritually.

Spiritual circumcision is the overcoming of the soul's basic instinct, of wanting to fulfil its unrighteous desire with the unrighteous mind, which then gives birth to unrighteous spirits. It is that type of mind that in the Book of Revelation is referred to as *the whore of Babylon*.

Logion 54

Jesus said, "Blessed are the poor, for yours is the kingdom of heaven."

Interpretation:

Blessed are the poor, for they are neither merchants nor businessmen who lust after the things of this world. Such souls will not enter the ***kingdom of heaven***.

Anyone can be wealthy and powerful in this world, but only if they are prepared to give up their empathy, and therefore their conscience first.

Is it not written **Mark 8:36** KJV: *For what shall it profit a man, if he shall gain the whole world, and lose his own soul?*

See also in **Matthew 5:3** KJV: *Blessed are the poor in spirit: for theirs is the kingdom of heaven.*

Logion 55

Jesus said, "Whoever does not hate his father and his mother cannot become a disciple to me. And whoever does not hate his brothers and sisters and take up his cross in my way will not be worthy of me."

Interpretation:

Whoever does not hate the unrighteous part of his desire (father), and the ignorant part of his mind (mother), *cannot become a disciple to me.*

And whoever does not hate his soul companions who have unrighteous desire and ignorant minds, and be prepared to suffer and be sacrificed *in my way will not be worthy of;* the Way, the Truth, and the Life.

Logion 56

Jesus said, "Whoever has come to understand the world has found (only) a corpse, and whoever has found a corpse is superior to the world."

Interpretation:

Whoever has come to understand the world will have realized that there is no Spirit of Understanding in it.

It is the Spirit that gives Life, and so without the Spirit, all that remains is that which is *a corpse*.

Whoever has within them the Spirit of Understanding has Life, and that which has life *is superior* to that which does not.

The dead rule this outer world, but the living rule their own inner world.

Logion 57

Jesus said, "The kingdom of the father is like a man who had good seed. His enemy came by night and sowed weeds among the good seed. The man did not allow them to pull up the weeds; he said to them, 'I am afraid that you will go intending to pull up the weeds and pull up the wheat along with them.' For on the day of the harvest the weeds will be plainly visible, and they will be pulled up and burned."

Interpretation:

This logion is a shortened version of the parable of the tares (weeds) of the field. The full version is recorded in the Gospel of **Matthew 13:24-30** KJV.

In **Matthew 13:36** KJV the multitudes were sent away and the disciples then asked Jesus to declare (make clear) to them the parable of the tares.

In **Matthew 23:37-39** KJV Jesus makes clear seven aspects of the parable: *He answered and said unto them, He that soweth the good seed is the Son of man; The field is the world; the good seed are the children of the kingdom; but the tares are the children of the wicked one; The enemy that sowed them is the devil; the harvest is the end of the world; and the reapers are the angels.*

We can now look at each of those aspects separately and

I will reveal their meanings.

   1. *He that soweth the good seed is the Son of man;*

The Son of man is a reference to the soul that is the first and True Image of the Self. It is the image of Truth, righteous desire, and Understanding. It is the True Image of the Self as a God, and that image is referred to as a soul.

Jesus was the Truth, and his teachings were the seeds of Truth. When those seeds were received by souls that possessed righteous desire, they too grew in Love, Truth and Understanding and became sons of God.

In John 1:12-13 KJV it is written: *But as many as received him, to them gave he power to become the sons of God, even to them that believe on his name:*

   2. *The field is the world*

The field is the surface of the subconscious mind, it exists within, and that surface is the place where the lower part of the conscious mind ends. This lower part of the conscious mind is the domain that the Self's soul was given to rule over. The inner spiritual world is likened to the material world, which is divided into three. There is the earth, the atmosphere and the space above the atmosphere.

   3. *the good seed are the children of the kingdom.*

The good seed are the souls that have received the seeds of Truth and have themselves become the Truth. They are the children of the kingdom of heaven. They are the children of the Self's righteous desire and the enlightened mind.

4. *the tares are the children of the wicked one*

The tares are the children of unrighteous desire and the ignorant mind that has no Light of Understanding. They are not a True Image of the Self.

5. *The enemy that sowed them is the devil*

The devil is a reference to unrighteous desire, which exists in the divided heart.

6. *the harvest is the end of the world*

The end of the world is the end of the soul's journey of learning; a journey in search of Truth and Understanding. **The harvest** is the gathering in of knowledge, which is food for the soul. It is a time of judgement where good is separated from evil, a time of choice where all things become undivided once more. It is the end of the tribulation. It is where the final battle ends and the soul becomes the conqueror.

7. *the reapers are the angels*

It is fitting that this is the seventh, because it is about the Self's and the souls righteous spirits (**angels**). They are the spirits that each give their Light of Truth to the soul, thereby enlightening it and giving it everlasting Life.

In logion 40 to 43 speaks of how the soul is filled with

righteous passion and how that passion burns up all that is not good and right in its kingdom.

The souls that are the children of unrighteous desire will be exposed to all, and their reign of unrighteousness will be ended. They will be left with nothing and no-one to deceive. Their wailing and gnashing of teeth will be because they will realize that their souls will be extinguished after they leave their physical bodies, therefore their whole life journey was worthless.

Whoever has the Spirit of Understanding let him understand.

Logion 58

Jesus said, "Blessed is the man who has suffered and found life."

Interpretation:

Unfulfilled desire is the cause of all the soul's sufferings and the most difficult of desires for the soul to fulfil is the desire for Understanding.

Blessed is the soul that has questioned the knowledge that he has and has found Understanding (***life***).

Cursed is the soul that has not questioned the knowledge that he has, and therefore is content with ignorance, and therefore death.

If you seek and continue seeking you will suffer along the way, but you will find Understanding (***life***).

Faith in knowledge without Understanding is no more than blind faith, and it is the soul that is blinded. Blind faith is no more than a crutch for the spiritually crippled.

If those who teach you prevent you from questioning the knowledge that they give you, then it is not to Life that they lead you but to death.

Truth has no fear of questioning. Neither do those who understand it.

Life is worth suffering for, death is not.

Seek and you will find.

See also in **1 Peter 4:1** KJV: *Forasmuch then as Christ hath suffered for us in the flesh, arm yourselves likewise with the same mind: for he that hath suffered in the flesh hath ceased from sin.*

Logion 59

Jesus said, "Take heed of the living one while you are alive, lest you die and seek to see him and be unable to do so."

Interpretation:

Pay attention to righteous desire *while you* have understanding, lest you lose your understanding *and seek to see him and be unable to do so.*

It is when the soul loses its understanding that it begins to question whether righteous desire is of benefit or a hindrance to the soul. It can no longer discern the value of Love or why it believed in it.

It is when the soul seeks the understanding of righteous desire which it once possessed that the dark night of the soul begins.

The question that the soul seeks an answer to is; was I a fool for putting the souls of others before my own pleasure and possessions, or was it the right thing to do? Did I suffer for nothing or for something?

Look at this world the way it is and what it should be like, and logic alone will make you realize that Love is the only Way.

Logion 60

<They saw> a Samaritan carrying a lamb on his way to Judea. He said to his disciples, "That man is round about the lamb." They said to him, "So that he may kill it and eat it." He said to them, "While it is alive, he will not eat it, but only when he has killed it and it has become a corpse." They said to him, "He cannot do so otherwise." He said to them, "You too, look for a place for yourself within repose, lest you become a corpse and be eaten."

Interpretation of:

This logion is quite big and so I will break it down and explain each part separately.

<They saw> a Samaritan carrying a lamb on his way to Judea.

Samaritans are described as:

Guardians/Keepers/Watchers of the Torah/Law. In other words; The Old Testament.

The lamb is likened to the Spirit of Understanding.

Judea is a reference to the Kingdom, whose capital is Jerusalem. It is likened to the Kingdom of Heaven and the New Jerusalem that will come down from Heaven.

Interpretation of:

He said to his disciples, "That man is round about the lamb."

This means that the soul of the Samaritan was embracing the Spirit of Understanding.

Interpretation of:

They said to him, "So that he may kill it and eat it."

Notice that this was not a question, it was a statement.

The disciples knew that the Samaritan had already consumed the knowledge of the Old Testament scriptures, (the Word) and it had become part of his soul, but the Samaritan had not yet consumed the Spirit of Understanding, which gives life to the Word.

The disciples knew that the only reason the Samaritan was carrying the Spirit of Understanding was so that he could **kill it and eat it**. This is because he was unable to comprehend the Light of Understanding in the Spirit, and so that Light which is the Life would have to be removed before he could consume it, and make it a part of his soul.

Interpretation of:

He said to them, "While it is alive, he will not eat it, but only when he has killed it and it has become a corpse."

While the Spirit of Understanding contains the Light of Life, the Samaritan will not be able to consume it, because it would cause a conflict with his materialistic beliefs. Only when he has removed the Light from the Understanding and it has ***become a corpse*** (dead) will he be able to consume it and make it a part of his soul.

The Word is the Truth, but it is the Spirit of Understanding that gives Life to the Word. Life can only come from Life, and so that which does not possess Life is dead.

Every soul and every spirit is regarded as dead if it does not possess the Light of Understanding, and those who are unable to see the Light are regarded as **blind**.

Of what worth is any knowledge or any soul without the Spirit of Understanding?

Interpretation of:

They said to him, "He cannot do so otherwise."

The disciples understood and they were in agreement.

Interpretation of:

He said to them, "You too, look for a place for yourself within repose, lest you become a corpse and be eaten."

The **place within** where **repose** (rest) is found is in the soul that possesses Truth and Understanding. Without the Spirit of Understanding the soul **becomes a corpse** that is **eaten** by death. So the message is; look within your soul for understanding.

Logion 61

Jesus said, "Two will rest on a bed: the one will die, and the other will live." Salome said, "Who are you, man that you ... have come up on my couch and eaten from my table?" Jesus said to her, "I am he who exists from the undivided. I was given some of the things of my father." <...> "I am your disciple." <...> "Therefore I say, if he is destroyed, he will be filled with light, but if he is divided, he will be filled with darkness."

Interpretation:

The two that rest on a bed are the two sons of the divided father. One son is born of the Self's righteous desire, and the other son is born of the Self's unrighteous desire.

It is the righteous son that possesses the Spirit of Understanding that lives, and it is the unrighteous son that possesses the spirit of ignorance that dies. It is the Spirit of Understanding that gives Life.

The *bed* that the *two rest on* is the *bed* of faith. The two sons each have faith in their respective fathers. The good son has faith in Love and seeks only pleasure in what is good and right.

The unrighteous son seeks pleasure by any means possible.

The good son has empathy and so understanding, therefore he has a conscience and feels guilt for causing hurt to others.

The bad son has no empathy and so cannot feel what others are feeling. Because of this he has no conscience and no feelings of guilt, he is the son of the devil, i.e. the evil heart; the tempter.

Salome is the spirit of peace, her *couch* is her resting place. That which is *eaten* from her *table* is the knowledge that brings contentment.

To *exist from the undivided* is to exist from the beginning when the Self's desire was undivided. It was a time when Jesus was given Love, Truth and Understanding (the Way, the Truth and the life).

<...> = Salome said to Jesus, *"I am your disciple."* This meant that peace was with Jesus as a follower and companion.

<...> = Jesus said to Salome.

The last part of the logion speaks of the Self's divided heart that has resulted in two fathers and two sons, one father and son being righteous, and the other father and son being unrighteous.

If unrighteous desire *is destroyed* then the whole heart *will be filled with light*. But as long as the heart is divided the whole heart *will be filled with darkness*.

Now this leaves a problem, because you cannot just stop one side of the heart without stopping the other. Therefore to stop desire completely requires the sacrifice of a son i.e. a soul. When one son is sacrificed its father simply stops, resulting in the whole heart stopping. All desire then ceases, both righteous and unrighteous desire. But which son is prepared to make such a sacrifice? It can only be the one who was there in the beginning, the Self's first and true soul, the one that was *given some of the things of* his *father*, i.e. righteous desire, in other words; the faithful son.

Listen and understand:

When a cup of wine is contaminated it must be emptied and washed before putting new wine in it. Likewise if the Self's desire is contaminated then Self's heart must be emptied and washed before putting righteous desire into it.

Desire must be silenced and no pleasure sought, not even the pleasure of life. It is unfulfilled desire that takes away peace.

The Self is immortal and cannot cease to exist. You existed even before you awoke to the realization of your existence, and in that moment of awakening your desire was silent, your heart was empty of want. It is to that moment in the beginning that you must return.

Your soul is no longer your Self's true image, and to restore that image and come to know yourself once more, you must silence your desire which will then no longer sustain any images that you have of yourself.

See also in **Luke 17:34 KJV:** *I tell you, in that night there shall be two men in one bed; the one shall be taken, and the other shall be left.*

Logion 62

Jesus said, "It is to those who are worthy of my mysteries that I tell my mysteries. Do not let your left (hand) know what your right (hand) is doing."

Interpretation:

Those who are worthy of my mysteries are the souls born of righteous desire. They are the ones who can comprehend the light of Truth, they are the children of righteous desire, and because they have understanding of spiritual things, they are referred to as *the living*. The children of unrighteous desire are unable to comprehend the light, they have no understanding of spiritual things and so they are referred to as *the dead.*

It is the hands that do the will of desire. Think of the two hands as the two opposing souls that do the will of their respective fathers. ***The left hand*** does the will of the unrighteous father, and ***the right hand*** does the will of the righteous father.

A righteous soul should not share its teachings with an unrighteous soul. This is because they will not understand, and they will either reject your teachings as foolish, or they will attack you.

Avoid inner conflict.

See also in **Matthew 13:10-13** KJV: *And the disciples came, and said unto him, Why speakest thou unto them in parables? He answered and said unto them, Because it is given unto you to know the mysteries of the kingdom of heaven, but to them it is not given. For whosoever hath, to him shall be given, and he shall have more abundance: but whosoever hath not, from him shall be taken away even that he hath. Therefore speak I to them in parables: because they seeing see not; and hearing they hear not, neither do they understand.*

Logion 63

Jesus said, "There was a rich man who had much money. He said, 'I shall put my money to use so that I may sow, reap, plant, and fill my storehouse with produce, with the result that I shall lack nothing.' Such were his intentions, but that same night he died. Let him who has ears hear."

Interpretation:

The *man* was wealthy and so should have been content with what he had, but there arose a desire within him for even more wealth for himself. In other words, he became greedy and selfish, and in the darkness of his ignorance he experienced death. There was no Light of Understanding left in him, and therefore he was left without a conscience, empathy and guilt. His intention alone was enough to extinguish any light within him.

Logion 64

Jesus said, "A man had received visitors. And when he had prepared the dinner, he sent his servant to invite the guests. He went to the first one and said to him, 'My master invites you.' He said, 'I have claims against some merchants. They are coming to me this evening. I must go and give them my orders. I ask to be excused from the dinner.' He went to another and said to him, 'My master has invited you.' He said to him, 'I have just bought a house and am required for the day. I shall not have any spare time.' He went to another and said to him, 'My master invites you.' He said to him, 'My friend is going to get married, and I am to prepare the banquet. I shall not be able to come. I ask to be excused from the dinner.' He went to another and said to him, 'My master invites you.' He said to him, 'I have just bought a farm, and I am on my way to collect the rent. I shall not be able to come. I ask to be excused.' The servant returned and said to his master, 'Those whom you invited to the dinner have asked to be excused.' The master said to his servant, 'Go outside to the streets and bring back those whom you happen to meet, so that they may dine.' Businessmen and merchants will not enter the places of my father."

Interpretation:

The *man* who *had received visitors* was Jesus.

The *visitor*s were those who were there for his teachings.

The *dinner* that was prepared was food for their soul, i.e. bread and wine.

Of the four *guests* that Jesus *sent his servant to invite*, the first two were *businessmen* and the other two were *merchants*. All four turned down the invitation because their desire for material things was greater than their desire for spiritual things.

Jesus then *sent his servant* out to invite people who were not *businessmen or merchants*.

Those whose desires are for the things of the world such as wealth and power, will not enter the places of righteous desire. They cannot serve two masters, i.e. they cannot serve righteous desire and unrighteous desire.

See also **Luke 14:16-24** KJV. *Then said he unto him, A certain man made a great supper, and bade many: And sent his servant at supper time to say to them that were bidden, Come; for all things are now ready. And they all with one consent began to make excuse. The first said unto him, I have bought a piece of ground, and I must needs go and see it: I pray thee have me excused. And* *another said, I have bought five yoke of oxen, and I go to prove them: I pray thee have me excused. And another said, I have married a wife, and therefore I cannot come. So that servant came, and shewed his lord these things. Then the master of the house being angry said to his servant, Go out quickly into the streets and lanes of the city, and bring in hither the poor, and the maimed, and the halt, and the blind. And the servant said, Lord, it is done as thou hast commanded, and yet there is room. And the lord said unto the servant, Go out into the highways and hedges, and compel them to come in, that my house may be filled. For I say unto you, That none of those men which were bidden shall taste of my supper.*

Logion 65

He said, "There was a good man who owned a vineyard. He leased it to tenant farmers so that they might work it and he might collect the produce from them. He sent his servant so that the tenants might give him the produce of the vineyard. They seized his servant and beat him, all but killing him. The servant went back and told his master. The master said, 'Perhaps he did not recognize them.' He sent another servant. The tenants beat this one as well. Then the owner sent his son and said, 'Perhaps they will show respect to my son.' Because the tenants knew that it was he who was the heir to the vineyard, they seized him and killed him. Let him who has ears hear."

Interpretation:

The ***good man who owned a vineyard*** was the father (the Self's righteous desire)

The ***vineyard*** is the place where the seeds of Self knowledge were planted.

The ***tenant farmers*** were the 7 *Spirits of God sent into all the earth* (subconscious mind). Each spirit leads a congregation of lesser spirits to assist them with nurturing the vines, and producing the fruit from which the pleasure of Self-knowledge would be gained.

The 7 Spirits of God are referred to as Angels, and the congregations of the lesser spirits are referred to as Churches.

The *first servant* that the father sent was the Spirit of righteous desire.

The *second servant* was the Spirit of Understanding.

The righteous father then sent *his son* who was created in the image of the father. The angels at this point had fallen from grace and had become the servants of the unrighteous father (the Devil) and the unrighteous son (Satan). At this point the Self's desire and mind had become divided.

They knew that the righteous son was *the heir* to the vineyard, (the Messiah, the faithful Son of righteous desire) and so not wanting to lose their power and worldly wealth, *they seized him and killed* the righteous son.

Let him who has the Spirit of Truth understand.

See also in **Matthew 21:33-39** KJV: *Hear another parable: There was a certain householder, which planted a vineyard, and hedged it round about, and digged a winepress in it, and built a tower, and let it out to husbandmen, and went into a far country:*

And when the time of the fruit drew near, he sent his servants to the husbandmen, that they might receive the fruits of it. And the husbandmen took his servants, and beat one, and killed another, and stoned another.Again, he sent other servants more than the first: and they did unto them likewise. But last of all he sent unto them his son, saying, They will reverence my son. But when the husbandmen saw the son, they said among themselves, This is the heir; come, let us kill him, and let us seize on his inheritance. And they caught him, and cast him out of the vineyard, and slew him.

> ## Logion 66
>
> Jesus said, "Show me the stone which the builders have rejected. That one is the cornerstone."

Interpretation:

The **cornerstone** is the first to be laid in the building of the soul's temple on earth. This stone is the first Truth by which all other Truths are measured for accuracy. That first Truth is knowledge of the Self as a spiritual being; it is this Truth that was **rejected**. That is why Jesus was rejected by the chief priests and Pharisees. A **stone** is a Truth.

See also in **Mark 12:10** KJV: *And have ye not read this scripture; The stone which the builders rejected is become the head of the corner:*

Logion 67

Jesus said, "If one who knows the all still feels a personal deficiency, he is completely deficient."

Interpretation:

The all is a reference to the kingdom within, i.e. the Self's spiritual domain. It is also referred to as the Self's mind. The mind is first and foremost a place that exists separately from the physical/material realm, and it is a completely different substance. It is the place that the Self has created and rules over, including over all things that are in its domain.

To know this and yet feel *a personal deficiency* means that you are *completely deficient.*

It is feelings of not being worthy, guilt and lack of Love for the Self that make you feel *deficient*. The soul cannot transcend into the higher mind while wearing garments of condemnation. It is Love, Truth and Understanding that allows the soul to remove its garments of condemnation and transcend.

Logion 68

Jesus said, "Blessed are you when you are hated and persecuted. Wherever you have been persecuted they will find no place."

Interpretation:

Those who are loving and speak the Truth, are hated and persecuted by those who have neither. Those who suffer hate and persecution for Love and Truth are blessed, for they shall find the Kingdom. ***Wherever you have been persecuted, they will find no place*** of repose (rest).

See also in **Matthew 5:10-12 KJV:** *Blessed are they which are persecuted for righteousness' sake: for theirs is the kingdom of heaven.*

Logion 69

Jesus said, "Blessed are they who have been persecuted within themselves. It is they who have truly come to know the father. Blessed are the hungry, for the belly of him who desires will be filled."

Interpretation:

Blessed are they who have a conscience and suffer for it, because that suffering is true repentance. It can only occur in loving souls who possess righteous desire, and in knowing righteous desire, ***the father*** is also known.

Blessed are those who are ***hungry*** for Truth and search for it, with righteous desire, for their hunger will be satisfied.

The bread of life is knowledge of Truth, which is food for the soul. What does it profit anyone that their physical body is satisfied and yet their soul is starving?

See also in **Matthew 5:10-12** KJV: *Blessed are they which are persecuted for righteousness' sake: for theirs is the kingdom of heaven.*

Logion 70

Jesus said, "That which you have will save you if you bring it forth from yourselves. That which you do not have within you will kill you if you do not have it within you."

Interpretation:

Righteous desire *will save* your soul if you have faith in it and express it.

If *you do not have* righteous desire within you, then all you have is unrighteous desire, and it is that which causes the *death* of the soul.

The absence of righteous desire is caused by the absence of Truth and the Light of Understanding. Without the light there is only the darkness of ignorance in which *death* is experienced.

Logion 71

Jesus said, "I shall destroy this house, and no one will be able to build it [...]."

Interpretation:

It is made clear in **John 2:19-21** KJV that when Jesus spoke of the temple he was speaking of the temple of his body.

When Jesus spoke these words he was speaking of sacrificing his spiritual body; his soul and no-one would be able to resurrect it. Only Love, Truth and Understanding could do that. These things are the Way, the Truth and the Life which form the perfected soul.

See in **John 2:19-21** KJV: *Jesus answered and said unto them, Destroy this temple, and in three days I will raise it up.*

See also in **Matthew 24:2-4** *And Jesus said unto them, See ye not all these things? verily I say unto you, There shall not be left here one stone upon another, that shall not be thrown down.*

Logion 72

A man said to him, "Tell my brothers to divide my father's possessions with me." He said to him, "O man, who has made me a divider?" He turned to his disciples and said to them, "I am not a divider, am I?"

Interpretation:

It is the *father* only who has the authority to judge the distribution of his possessions to his children. The *man* wasn't left anything to inherit, and so he was coveting his *brother's* inheritance. The brother's father had not given Jesus any authority to judge who gets what, so he was not made *a divider*.

This logion relates to **Luke 12:13-15** KJV, which is followed by a parable, explaining that you cannot take worldly possessions with you when you leave this world, and so they have no worth to the soul.

Luke 12:13-15 KJV: *And one of the company said unto him, Master, speak to my brother, that he divide the inheritance with me. And he said unto him, Man, who made me a judge or a divider over you? And he said unto them, Take heed, and beware of covetousness: for a man's life consisteth not in the abundance of the things which he possesseth.*

Logion 73

Jesus said, "The harvest is great but the laborers are few. Beseech the Lord, therefore, to send out laborers to the harvest."

Interpretation:

The harvest is Truth, and *the laborers* are the soul's seven spirits of Understanding (*angels*) that reap the Truth and give life to it.

The harvest happens at the end of the soul's world within, it is the time of the soul's death and rebirth that results in enlightenment and transcendence.

See also in **Matthew 19:37** KJV: *Then saith he unto his disciples, The harvest truly is plenteous, but the labourers are few.*

Logion 74

He said, "O Lord, there are many around the drinking trough, but there is nothing in the cistern."

Interpretation:

Jesus was referring here to the temple where the blind guides were teaching the Law/Word, without the Spirit.

In scriptures knowledge is food, and water is spirit.

Logion 75

Jesus said, "Many are standing at the door, but it is the solitary who will enter the bridal chamber."

Interpretation:

The door represents a doorway in the mind that leads the soul into paradise, (Heaven) which is the higher mind. It is also *the bridle chamber* where the soul becomes the groom to the righteous mind, and the two become one once more.

'When you stand alone (solitary), with nothing that the world can take from you, and only Love in your heart, it is then that the doorway to heaven will open for you.' William.

Logion 76

Jesus said, "The kingdom of the father is like a merchant who had a consignment of merchandise and who discovered a pearl. That merchant was shrewd. He sold the merchandise and bought the pearl alone for himself. You too, seek his unfailing and enduring treasure where no moth comes near to devour and no worm destroys."

Interpretation:

The kingdom of the father is the mind. The *merchant* is of course a reference to the soul that exists within and is a part of the mind.

The *merchandise* is of course the knowledge contained in the mind.

There is a general misunderstanding that pearls represent wisdom, but anyone who has read Job 28 KJV in the Bible would know that wisdom is far more precious than pearls, gold or precious stones.

A *pearl* represents a Truth hidden and growing in the darkness, and until it is discovered and brought into the light, it will remain a mystery.

A pearl begins forming when a piece of grit enters the oyster and begins irritating it. Likewise when a Truth enters the subconscious mind and remains hidden, it will irritate the Self until it is discovered and brought into the Light of Understanding in the conscious mind, where it will reveal its beauty and worth.

Interpreting scriptures is like opening oysters, some are difficult and you never know what you will find.

The *pearl* that the *merchant* found was knowledge of the Self, and that knowledge was worth more than all the other knowledge contained in his mind.

Seek and you will find, and in finding you will have come to know yourself, and nothing will ever take that from you or harm that knowledge.

See also in **Matthew 13:44-46 KJV:** *Again, the kingdom of heaven is like unto treasure hid in a field; the which when a man hath found, he hideth, and for joy thereof goeth and selleth all that he hath, and buyeth that field. Again, the kingdom of heaven is like unto a merchant man, seeking goodly pearls: Who, when he had found one pearl of great price, went and sold all that he had, and bought it.*

Logion 77

Jesus said, "It is I who am the light which is above them all. It is I who am the all. From me did the all come forth, and unto me did the all extend. Split a piece of wood, and I am there. Lift up the stone, and you will find me there."

This logion contains six statements, so I will separate and interpret them one at a time.

Interpretation of:

It is I who am the light which is above them all.

In this material world it is the Sun that is the light above us all, likewise in the spiritual world within (the mind), it is the light of the Father, (the Self's righteous desire) that is above all that is in the mind. The symbol of the Father is the Sun. It has been used throughout history.

It is because the soul of Jesus was one with the Father that he could also say; *I am the light which is above them all.*

Interpretation of:

It is I who am the all. From me did the all come forth

The soul of Jesus and every other spiritual being is formed within and from the substance of the mind.

It is the mind that is referred to as *the all*.

Interpretation of:

From me did the all come forth

The soul is the Self's image in the mind, and in the beginning that image existed in a state of righteous desire, and it was from that image that *the all came forth*.

The soul was given dominion over the inner world to create and use according to its desire. Therefore everything within the soul's domain came *forth* from the soul.

It is the soul that manifests all that is in its domain (mind) and they are manifested for its own pleasure.

Interpretation of:

and unto me did the all extend.

Everything that the soul creates in the mind comes back to affect the soul, like an echo. The soul reaps what it sows. It is wise to sow only what is good and right.

Interpretation of:

Split a piece of wood, and I am there.

Wood comes from trees, and in spiritual terms *wood* represents knowledge. This is why Jesus was referred to as carpenter. So *split a piece of wood* means finding the Truth in knowledge. *Jesus said; 'I am the Way, the TRUTH, and the Life'*. You see the Truth can be found in the soul of Jesus.

Interpretation of:

Lift up the stone, and you will find me there."

In spiritual terms a *stone* represents a Truth.

The cornerstone of the soul's temple is one of Truth, and it is by this *stone* that the rest of the temple is made accurate, strong and perfect. It is the most important stone in any building.

Beneath that stone are the foundations on which it is laid. They are the foundations of understanding, and when the understanding is solid and immovable they are referred to spiritually as rock.

It is understanding that supports and gives life to the Truth. It is *upon this rock* that Jesus built his church.

There is no greater faith found in a soul than one who has both Truth and Understanding.

See also in **John 8:12 KJV:** *Then spake Jesus again unto them, saying, I am the light of the world: he that followeth me shall not walk in darkness, but shall have the light of life.*

Logion 78

Jesus said, "Why have you come out into the desert? To see a reed shaken by the wind? And to see a man clothed in fine garments like your kings and your great men? Upon them are the fine garments, and they are unable to discern the truth."

Interpretation:

The desert is a place of sand, a place where Truth has no solid foundations, a place hostile to life. Jesus was of course thinking about the temple and its teachers.

They who came to listen to him were expecting to see a man *shaken by the wind*s of desire, a man dressed *in fine garments* of power. Such men could not even understand the Truth.

People should not judge a man's worth by the worldly clothes that he wears, but rather by his spiritual clothes.

See also in **Matthew 11:7-14 KJV:** *And as they departed, Jesus began to say unto the multitudes concerning John, What went ye out into the wilderness to see? A reed shaken with the wind? But what went ye out for to see? A man clothed in soft raiment? behold, they that wear soft clothing are in kings' houses.*

Logion 79

A woman from the crowd said to him, "Blessed are the womb which bore you and the breasts which nourished you." He said to her, "Blessed are those who have heard the word of the father and have truly kept it. For there will be days when you will say, 'Blessed are the womb which has not conceived and the breasts which have not given milk.'"

Interpretation:

In adoration of Jesus *the woman from the crowd* praises his mother. Jesus replies by praising his *father*.

For those who have not *heard the word of the father or kept it*, there will be days for those like the woman from the crowd, when they will wish they had not been born.

It can be seen even today in the church that the Mother and the Son are praised much more than the Father, and indeed it is the priests who have taken the name father for themselves in defiance of the scriptures.

See also in **Luke 23:29** KJV: *For, behold, the days are coming, in the which they shall say, Blessed are the barren, and the wombs that never bare, and the paps which never gave suck.*

Logion 80

Jesus said, "He who has recognized the world has found the body, but he who has found the body is superior to the world."

Interpretation:

To *recognize* this material world is to become aware of what exists outside of the space that your physical body occupies. Therefore *recognizing the world* also leads to finding the physical body.

Likewise: To recognize the spiritual world within (the mind) is to become aware of what exists outside of the space that your spiritual body (soul) occupies. Therefore recognizing the mind also leads to finding your soul.

He who has found the physical body is superior to the material world.

Likewise: *He who has found the* spiritual body (soul) *is superior* to the spiritual world (mind).

Contemplate the following for each world:

I am here, that is there

I am the observer, not that which I observe.

I am the thinker, not the thought.

I am that I am and not that which exists outside of I.

I am the creator and ruler of my own inner world.

Self over mind; Mind over matter.

Logion 81

Jesus said, "Let him who has grown rich be king, and let him who possesses power renounce it."

Interpretation:

Let the soul *who has grown rich* with knowledge of Truth *be king, and let* the soul that *possesses* such *power* give it up to the father.

The soul's father is of course the Self's righteous desire, which is the creator and ruler that sits on the Throne in Heaven (the righteous mind).

See also in **Luke 14:33 KJV** *So likewise, whosoever he be of you that forsaketh not all that he hath, he cannot be my disciple.*

Logion 82

Jesus said, "He who is near me is near the fire, and he who is far from me is far from the kingdom."

Interpretation:

He who is near to the Christ soul within *is near the fire* (passion) of righteous desire.

He who is far from the Christ within *is far from the kingdom* of heaven.

Logion 83

Jesus said, "The images are manifest to man, but the light in them remains concealed in the image of the light of the father. He will become manifest, but his image will remain concealed by his light."

Interpretation:

The images spoken of here are images of spiritual entities. We all present an image of ourselves to others. Those images are sometimes hidden behind a mask and so present a false image of the soul.

The images that are made *manifest to man* are images of our own soul and the souls of other. In scripture *man* is a reference to the soul.

The soul is not the Self, it is an image that the Self has formed to represent the Self, and that image exists in the mind.

In beginning when the Self awakened and became Self-aware, it formed a perfect image of itself. The image that you now have of your Self has become corrupted and needs to be made perfect again, it is why you do not understand who and what you really are anymore. This is why it was said; *you must come to know yourself.*

The father represents your souls creator, in other words, your soul was created by your Self's righteous desire, and it was created at the beginning of your Self's life journey when you were full of the Light of Understanding.

The Light of Understanding in your soul now is weak and your true light ***remains concealed in the*** light of your Self's righteous desire.

You ***will become*** one with the Self's righteous desire, but your true ***image will remain concealed by his light***.

To become enlightened is like going back to the beginning and being born again. Your whole mind will be filled with the Light of Understanding, and your whole being will be permeated with the perfect Love of righteous desire.

Have you ever wondered why the Holy Trinity is; Father, Son and Holy Ghost, and does not include God?

It is because the **father** is the Self's righteous desire.

The **son** is the Self's image of itself.

And the **holy spirit** is the Self's Spirit of Understanding and so it is the Spirit of Truth, the comforter.

What they don't want people to realize is that <u>you are a GOD</u>, you are a creator, because if you did realize you would have found the Truth that sets you free.

You are immortal, and your soul came from the Light, and to the light your soul will return. I see you.

Logion 84

Jesus said, "When you see your likeness, you rejoice. But when you see your images which came into being before you, and which neither die nor become manifest, how much you will have to bear!"

Interpretation:

I want you to look inside your mind and ask yourself; what am I like? It is then that *you* will *see* a reflection of the image of your soul; a *likeness* of yourself. Many are afraid to do this because they fear what they will see. This is because they have accepted the judgements of others who have made them feel unworthy of Love and respect. This causes feelings of guilt and shame resulting in low self-esteem. On the other hand, there are those who have no fear of looking at their likeness, this is because they have come to believe they are worthy of Love and respect.

Neither of these two types are a true image of the Self. What you see is what you have come to believe.

The disciples of Jesus had come to believe that they were righteous, but they had become prideful, so Jesus gave them a warning.

When the image of the Self's soul first came into being on the 6th day it was a perfect image of the Self. But when the Self's image came into being once more on the 8th day, its corruption followed.

The Self's first and true image cannot die because the Self cannot *die*, and it cannot become *manifest* because there is no darkness in it to form an image.

Images are formed from darkness and light, and so when the image of the soul forms in the mind it means there is still darkness in the mind.

When the disciples realize this they will realize that compared to the Self's first and true image, they are imperfect and far from grace. *How much* then will they *have to bear* as their pride falls.

Both the Self's true soul and mind are filled with light, and so they are hidden as they are *the light* within the light.

The Self's soul came from the light, and to the light it will return. We are the children of the light.

The scriptures always showed the way to enlightenment; the way home.

Logion 85

Jesus said, "Adam came into being from a great power and a great wealth, but he did not become worthy of you. For had he been worthy, he would not have experienced death."

Interpretation:

The *great power* and *great wealth* that *Adam came into being from* was of course the Self's righteous desire (unconditional Love) and the Truth (the Word).

The first form of the Self's soul was created in Heaven from the substance of the perfect conscious mind. The second form of the Self's soul was made from the substance of the Self's subconscious mind. Whenever you remember something you are recreating an image that first formed in the conscious mind.

Every child comes into the world with a remembrance of the Self's first image. They are innocent and possess only the attributes of righteous desire and the Truth of their existence. To recognize this in a new born child is to know the place of life.

Everyone begins their life journey with an *Adam* soul, but as we grow and learn knowledge of evil, the soul changes. To live without righteous desire, the Truth of what we are, and to be without understanding, is to *experience death*. Many people experience this without even realizing it.

Adam souls such as these are not worthy of the Self, and after a life journey, they are discarded and replaced with a new soul once more. If your soul has a good measure of Love, Truth, and Understanding, it is kept for another life journey. It is up to the Self whether or not the soul reincarnates. For those who achieve enlightenment there is eternal life for the soul.

The Self cannot cease to exist, but an Adam soul can.

How many life journeys will you suffer before you realize these things?

Logion 86

Jesus said, "The foxes have their holes and the birds have their nests, but the son of man has no place to lay his head and rest."

Interpretation:

Jesus once referred to Herod as a fox, so first of all we must consider the nature of a fox. *Foxes* are of course sly, which means that they are cunning and deceitful. They also creep about quietly and carefully so as not to be noticed. In the secret language of scriptures, foxes represent subconscious thoughts that possess the same nature as foxes, such thoughts are also referred to as *creeping things*. These thoughts are created by the Self's inner desires within the subconscious mind. It is when those inner desires are fulfilled that they rest. In scripture the Earth is a reference to the subconscious mind.

The *birds* are a reference to thoughts in the conscious mind, which in scripture is referred to as the sky. *Nests* are of course made in trees, and spiritually the trees are trees of knowledge. The nests are places where thoughts rest in their beliefs

The son of man is the Christ soul and *so has no place to rest* from his mission, there is no safe place for such a soul.

See also in **Matthew 8:20** KJV: *And Jesus saith unto him, The foxes have holes, and the birds of the air have nests; but the Son of man hath not where to lay his head.*

Logion 87

Jesus said, "Wretched is the body that is dependent upon a body, and wretched is the soul that is dependent on these two."

Interpretation:

The key to understanding this logion is in the realization that the mind is the Self's spiritual *body*.

Wretched is the spiritual *body* (mind) *that is dependent upon a* physical *body and wretched is the soul that is dependent on these two.*

That which is dependent is not free; it is in need of something that it doesn't have. Dependence results in the creation of attachments.

Enlightenment day is Independence day.

Sometimes you have to give in to win.

Logion 88

Jesus said, "The angels and the prophets will come to you and give to you those things you (already) have. And you too, give them those things which you have, and say to yourselves, 'When will they come and take what is theirs?'"

Interpretation:

In scripture *angels* represent the Spirits of Understanding that give life to the Word. *Prophets* are spirits of the Word. These entities do not exist within the soul, and that is why it is said, they *will come to you*. When Jesus was baptized the spirit descended upon him and when he spoke he said *the spirit is upon me*. The key word is 'upon' not 'within.'

It is angel and prophet entities that store the soul's treasure, and that is why it is said that *they will come to you and give you those things which you already have.*

The *things* that the soul has to give to the *angels and prophets* are Love, faith and righteousness. It is then that they will take their place in the resurrection.

Logion 89

Jesus said, "Why do you wash the outside of the cup? Do you not realize that he who made the inside is the same one who made the outside?"

Interpretation:

In scripture the *cup* represents the spiritual heart and the spiritual blood represents desire (which is also referred to as wine).

It is the Self that made the heart of the soul, and when it was made in the beginning it was filled with righteous desire. What does it profit a soul that his heart looks clean and yet it is filled with corruption?

First clean *the inside* of the cup then *the outside* will also be clean.

Do not be fooled by unrighteous desire clothed in a righteous looking heart.

See also in **Matthew 23:26** KJV: *Thou blind Pharisee, cleanse first that which is within the cup and platter, that the outside of them may be clean also.*

Logion 90

Jesus said, "Come unto me, for my yoke is easy and my lordship is mild, and you will find repose for yourselves."

Interpretation:

Spiritually a *yoke* is a reference to one's conscience. When we act against our conscience it becomes restrictive and oppressive, we then suffer from feelings of guilt and our peace is taken away. Jesus obeyed his conscience and did only what was good and right, he was gentle, kind and understanding, and his heart was righteous, having no desire for the things of this world. He was also a teacher and so was referred to as 'master', but he never forced his teachings on his students, in other words, his *lordship* was *mild*.

It is with such a teacher that students find *repose* and inner peace for themselves. In troubled times he would say to his students; *rest in my peace.*

See in **Matthew 11:28-30** KJV: *Come unto me, all ye that labour and are heavy laden, and I will give you rest. Take my yoke upon you, and learn of me; for I am meek and lowly in heart: and ye shall find rest unto your souls. For my yoke is easy, and my burden is light.*

Logion 91

They said to him, "Tell us who you are so that we may believe in you." He said to them, "You read the face of the sky and of the earth, but you have not recognized the one who is before you, and you do not know how to read this moment."

Interpretation:

It was not up to Jesus to say who he was, it was up to his students to realize for themselves, and at this point the students had much to learn and understand. If Jesus had said that he was the son of God then he would not be seen as humble, and he would only be claiming what others had previously claimed to be.

In scriptures *the sky* is likened to the conscious mind, and *the earth* is likened to the subconscious mind. It is *the face of the sky* that reveals what is to come (the future), and it is the face *of the earth* that reveals what was (the past). The student *had not recognized the one before them*, they had not recognized the soul that is. This is because they had not recognized their own souls, and so they did not know how to read the present *moment*.

It is the Self's True Image that is the Alpha and Omega, i.e. the first and the last, but there is also an in between, that is why the soul is described as; '*what is, what was, and what is to come*' in **Revelation 1:8** KJV.

Logion 92

Jesus said, "Seek and you will find. Yet, what you asked me about in former times and which I did not tell you then, now I do desire to tell, but you do not inquire after it."

Interpretation:

To *seek* is to search for understanding, and this is done by questioning and considering everything with an open mind. If we continue seeking we will eventually *find* what we are searching for, but if we stop seeking we will never find what we were searching for.

In former times the students asked many questions in their search for Truth and Understanding, but they were not then ready to grasp advanced teachings, and so they were not told things that were below their level of understanding at that time.

Now the students had reached a greater level of understanding and were ready to receive advanced teachings, but now they had stopped seeking a greater understanding and did not ask about those things that they asked about in former times.

It is when we stop questioning that we submit to ignorance.

Logion 93

<Jesus said,> "Do not give what is holy to dogs, lest they throw them on the dung-heap. Do not throw the pearls to swine, lest they [...] it [...]."

Interpretation:

That which is described as *holy* comes from the word 'whole.' The Truth without understanding is not whole, in other words, the Word without the Spirit of Understanding is not whole/holy. *The Word without the Spirit is a dead letter.*

Those who were given the authority to teach the Old Testament taught the Word but without the Spirit of Understanding, and by doing this they gained much power and wealth for themselves. They would not have had such things if they had given the Spirit of Understanding, which is the key that they hid from the people. Jesus described the temple authorities as a dog in a manger. It follows that the people that they indoctrinated also became like *dogs* and full of ignorance and pride, they are lovers of worldly things and are materialistic minded. If you speak to them of spiritual things that challenge their materialistic beliefs they will treat your words as nonsense, and they will turn on you.

People who are described as being *swine*/pigs, are people who only care about things that give them personal pleasure. They will do anything and believe anything if it makes them feel good. If it doesn't they will reject it. Such people are considered to be unclean.

Pearls are revelations of hidden truths.

See also in **Matthew 7:6** KJV: *Give not that which is holy unto the dogs, neither cast ye your pearls before swine, lest they trample them under their feet, and turn again and rend you.*

Logion 94

Jesus said, "He who seeks will find, and he who knocks will be let in."

Interpretation:

To *seek* is to search for something you don't have, but desire. It is plain to see that in Logion 1, the reader is encouraged to search for the interpretation of the secret sayings. If the reader keeps searching they will eventually find understanding.

The hands do the will of desire, and so to *knock* is to express the will of desire to enter the place of mysteries.

See also in **Matthew 7:7** KJV: *Ask, and it shall be given you; seek, and ye shall find; knock, and it shall be opened unto you:*

Logion 95

Jesus said, "If you have money, do not lend it at interest, but give it to one from whom you will not get it back."

Interpretation:

If you have money to *lend* then you already have more than you need.

You should not take advantage of those who are in need, by lending them money and charging them *interest*, because you make their struggle even greater. What then have you done for them that is good? You will do far more good by giving the money you do not need, to those who have less than they need, and your reward will be greater.

Logion 96

Jesus said, "The kingdom of the father is like a certain woman. She took a little leaven, concealed it in some dough, and made it into large loaves. Let him who has ears hear."

Interpretation:

In scripture *the kingdom* is a reference to the mind, which is ruled over by the Self's desire. It is the mind that is referred to as the kingdom within.

The father and the son, i.e. soul are always defined as being male, whereas the mind is described as being female.

When the Self's desire is divided it results in there being two minds, i.e. two kingdoms, one righteous and one unrighteous.

A certain woman is a reference to the mind of righteous desire.

Therefore the righteous mind *took a little leaven*, i.e. the spirit of wonder, and she *concealed it in some dough*.

Dough is flour and water, therefore spiritually this means Truth and the Spirit of Understanding. She then made them *into large loaves*, i.e. the bread of life, which is food for the hungry souls. Such food is given in parables to those who have the ears to hear.

See also in **Matthew 13:33** KJV: *Another parable He spoke to them: "The kingdom of heaven is like leaven, which a woman took and hid in three measures of meal till it was all leavened."*

Logion 97

Jesus said, "The kingdom of the father is like a certain woman who was carrying a jar full of meal. While she was walking on the road, still some distance from home, the handle of the jar broke and the meal emptied out behind her on the road. She did not realize it; she had noticed no accident. When she reached her house, she set the jar down and found it empty."

Interpretations:

Jesus said, "The kingdom of the father is like a certain woman

The kingdom of the father is of course the mind, and spiritually the mind is referred to as being female as in *woman*. Therefore this logion is referring to a certain type of mind.

who was carrying a jar full of meal.

The jar full of meal represents a place in the subconscious mind that holds memories of spiritual knowledge (*meal*) related to the beginning and nature of the mind.

While she was walking on the road, still some distance from home,

While traveling on its life journey, still some distance from its end.

the handle of the jar broke

The mind became distracted by the things of the material world, and its focus of attention (*handle*) on its spiritual memories broke.

and the meal emptied out behind her on the road.

The minds spiritual memories began pouring out and were left in the past and forgotten.

She did not realize it; she had noticed no accident.

The mind did not realize what was happening because its attention was on the things of the material world.

When she reached her house, she set the jar down and found it empty."

When the mind reached the end of its life journey and began looking back, it found no memories of its beginning or nature. It had no knowledge or understanding of its nature or why it even existed. Its journey had been wasted on the temporary, and the mind

178

that had become fully carnal had only oblivion in its future as all of its carnal memories were now worthless.

You too be careful and cling to spiritual Love, remember your beginning then you will have no fear of the end of this life journey. Seek the immortal not the temporary things.

Logion 98

Jesus said, "The kingdom of the father is like a certain man who wanted to kill a powerful man. In his own house he drew his sword and stuck it into the wall in order to find out whether his hand could carry through. Then he slew the powerful man."

Interpretation:

The kingdom of the father is the mind, and the soul is formed within and of the substance of the mind. The soul is an image of the Self, created by its desire and so desire is the father of the soul.

This logion speaks of two men/souls in one divided ***house***/mind.

In the beginning the Self's desire had only one son that was the Self's True Image, and it was righteous. But when desire became divided there were two fathers, one good and one unrighteous. The unrighteous desire is referred to as the devil. The unrighteous father also had a son, one filled with unrighteous desire and ignorance.

In this logion the righteous soul who is referred to as the son of God, is attempting to disempower the son of the devil. This is a battle that we all face in life, and it was one that Jesus faced when he encountered the Temple authorities.

The *sword* here is of course the two edged sword of Truth and Understanding, the Word and the Holy Spirit.

The wall is of course the resistance of the children of the devil.

It is Truth and Understanding that can penetrate the resistance of the minds and souls of the children of the devil, who are ignorant and full of unrighteous desire. They are the ones who love the things of the world and care only for themselves.

See also in **Matthew 4:1** KJV: *Then was Jesus led up of the Spirit into the wilderness to be tempted of the devil.*

Logion 99

The disciples said to him, "Your brothers and your mother are standing outside." He said to them, "Those here who do the will of my father are my brothers and my mother. It is they who will enter the kingdom of my father."

Interpretation:

Jesus did not consider his physical brothers and physical mother as his true family, he knew that he was a spiritual being, and that the mother of his soul was the mind of righteous desire. He considered those who were there with him already as his true **brothers and mother** because their souls too were born of the righteous mind, and did the will of righteous desire i.e. the father. All who do the will of righteous desire and are born of the righteous mind are of the same family who existed in the beginning and came from the light.

See also in **Matthew 12:46** KJV: *While he yet talked to the people, behold, his mother and his brethren stood without, desiring to speak with him. Then one said unto him, Behold, thy mother and thy brethren stand without, desiring to speak with thee. But he answered and said unto him that told him, Who is my mother? and who are my brethren? And he stretched forth his hand toward his disciples, and said, Behold my mother and my brethren!*

Logion 100

They showed Jesus a gold coin and said to him, "Caesar's men demand taxes from us." He said to them, "Give Caesar what belongs to Caesar, give God what belongs to God, and give me what is mine."

Interpretation:

Caesar was the ruler of this material world, and so all the material things of this world belonged to him.

God (the Self) is the ruler of its inner spiritual world, and so all spiritual things belonged to God.

That which belonged to Jesus was peace.

Caesar's men had conquered the world in the name of Caesar, but Jesus' spirits had conquered the world within in the name of God the Self.

See also in **Matthew 22:21** KJV: *They say unto him, Caesar's. Then saith he unto them, Render therefore unto Caesar the things which are Caesar's; and unto God the things that are God's.*

Logion 101

<Jesus said,> "Whoever does not hate his father and his mother as I do cannot become a disciple to me. And whoever does not love his father and his mother as I do cannot become a disciple to me. For my mother [...], but my true mother gave me life."

Interpretation:

This logion speaks of two fathers and two mothers. In other words; two desire and two minds. The result of this was a soul with a duel personality with one side struggling against the other in a battle for spiritual domination of the kingdom within.

In the beginning the soul knew only what was good and right and there was peace in the kingdom, but then the soul discovered knowledge of evil and everything became divided and peace ended. Jesus conquered the unrighteous part of his personality through Love, Truth and Understanding and set out to teach other souls how to do what he had done, choosing only those who had not fallen completely to their dark side.

Whoever did *not hate his* unrighteous desire and unrighteous mind could not *become a disciple to* him.

And whoever did ***not love*** his righteous desire and righteous mind could ***not become a disciple to*** him.

For his unrighteous mother gave him knowledge but his ***true mother gave*** him understanding.

See also in **Luke 14:26** KJV: *If any man come to me, and hate not his father, and mother, and wife, and children, and brethren, and sisters, yea, and his own life also, he cannot be my disciple.*

It is only the unrighteous that he taught people to hate, but he also taught that they should be forgiven because of his unconditional love and understanding.

Logion 102

Jesus said, "Woe to the Pharisees, for they are like a dog sleeping in the manger of oxen, for neither does he eat nor does he let the oxen eat."

Interpretation:

Pharisees are defined as members of an ancient Jewish sect, distinguished by strict observance of the traditional and written law. They were protecting the Word but they were sleeping in ignorance of the Spirit of Understanding. This resulted in the people only receiving a literal and materialistic interpretation of the Word.

Without the Spirit of Understanding the Word is a dead letter, in other words, there is no life in it. It is the Spirit that gives life to the Word. The Spirit of Understanding is the key they are said to have hidden.

The manger is a reference to the cradle of life. *Oxen* is a reference to spirits of righteous desire.

The Pharisees refused to *eat*/consume the Spirit of Understanding and they would not let the people consume it either. This is because if the people understood the true meanings of the scriptures the Pharisees would have been exposed as *blind guides.*

Logion 103

Jesus said, "Fortunate is the man who knows where the brigands will enter, so that he may get up, muster his domain, and arm himself before they invade."

Interpretation:

A *brigand* is defined as a member of a gang that ambushes and robs people.

The Pharisees tried many times with the use of scriptures to do a surprise attack on Jesus and his teachings, but Jesus had prepared his mind, and armed himself with scriptures for a counter attack. He knew what scriptures they would use and so was ready to defend himself and *his* inner *domain*/mind.

Those who teach a literal and therefore a materialistic version of the scriptures, will inevitably find themselves teaching conflicting scriptures, and they will find themselves in a place that they cannot defend, a place where even their own beliefs are in conflict with one another. This is the problem with Christianity today. So many have become like the Pharisees rather than a Christ.

Logion 104

They said to Jesus, "Come, let us pray today and let us fast." Jesus said, "What is the sin that I have committed, or wherein have I been defeated? But when the bridegroom leaves the bridal chamber, then let them fast and pray."

Interpretation:

Prayers are requests made to the Self's righteous desire. They are very personal and should be made in private by the soul. Therefore they are communications between the son and the father alone. The Lord's Prayer in **Matthew 6:9-13** KJV contains the only things that should be prayed for by the soul seeking its redemption.

Praying is required by those who have sinned, and those of little faith in the father.

Jesus had not sinned and so was not in need of forgiveness and he was full of faith.

Fasting is done to overcome the temptation of worldly desire. Jesus had not *been defeated* by such temptations. There was no need for him to *pray* or *fast.*

The bridegroom is a reference to the soul that is the son of righteous desire. The *bridal chamber* is the mind/kingdom of the father that was to be the son's inheritance. It is the place where *the two become one*; the Word and the Holy Spirit.

When the bridegroom leaves the bridal chamber it is like breaking an engagement vow and lusting for the unrighteous mind, because of lack of faith.

When the bridegroom leaves the chamber he enters the mind of unrighteous desire, which is the kingdom of the unrighteous heart. This is also known as the kingdom of the devil, i.e. hell.

See also in **Matthew 9:15** *And Jesus said unto them, Can the children of the bridechamber mourn, as long as the bridegroom is with them? but the days will come, when the bridegroom shall be taken from them, and then shall they fast.*

Logion 105

Jesus said, "He who knows the father and the mother will be called the son of a harlot."

Interpretation:

The soul that is familiar or friendly with unrighteous desire and the unrighteous mind will be called *the son of a harlot*.

The archaic definition of the word *harlot* is; a prostitute or promiscuous woman.

Origin: (denoting a vagabond or beggar, later a lecherous man or woman). It is also used to describe a 'young man' or 'knave.'

Logion 106

Jesus said, "When you make the two one, you will become the sons of man, and when you say, 'Mountain, move away,' it will move away."

Interpretation:

When you make the Word and the Holy Spirit ***one, you will become the sons of man, and when you say to the Mountain*** of despair, ***move away it will move away.***

The Word is the Truth. The Holy Spirit is the Spirit of Truth. The Spirit of Truth is the Light of Understanding. Without the Spirit of Understanding the Word is a dead letter; it has no power.

Without the Spirit of Understanding the heart (desire) becomes divided and set against itself. Each side engages in a battle for supremacy, because of this neither side can express its full power, which is willpower.

When the heart (desire) is divided, one side is full of the light of Truth and the other side is full of the darkness of ignorance.

When the righteous heart (desire) is undivided its will is fully empowered, and it is able once more to create or destroy whatever it chooses.

Have faith in Love, make it unconditional.

Have faith in Truth until the Spirit of Understanding comes, then your faith will become unbreakable, and you will rule over the ALL.

The Father becomes the Son, the Son becomes the Father.

There is only one way to the door of eternal life for the soul, and only one path. It is the path of faith in Unconditional Love, Truth and it is lit by the Light of Understanding.

See also in **Matthew 17:20** KJV: *And Jesus said unto them, Because of your unbelief: for verily I say unto you, If ye have faith as a grain of mustard seed, ye shall say unto this mountain, Remove hence to yonder place; and it shall remove; and nothing shall be impossible unto you.*

> ## Logion 107
>
> Jesus said, "The kingdom is like a shepherd who had a hundred sheep. One of them, the largest, went astray. He left the ninety-nine sheep and looked for that one until he found it. When he had gone to such trouble, he said to the sheep, 'I care for you more than the ninety-nine.'"

Interpretation:

The kingdom is of course the mind, and every mind contains a soul that is formed from the substance of mind. The kingdom is therefore inside of the soul and it is outside of the soul (see Logion 3).

The mind is a spiritual realm and so everything contained within it is of it, including the soul and all other spiritual entities.

In scripture all good souls are referred to as *sheep*, and evil souls are referred to as *wolves*.

Jesus' soul was referred to as a *lamb* and because he cared for and protected other souls he was referred to as *a shepherd*.

The soul that *went astray* was the soul of Mary Magdalene. Jesus cared for this soul more than other souls because he loved her. When he found her he rescued her from those who wanted to stone her, after which she would never go astray again. We guard those we love, but we guard those we are in love with even more.

Mary was the most worthy of the mysteries and she was closer to Jesus than any other disciple; she was his soulmate.

See The Gospel of Mary Fully Interpreted and the truth that has been hidden from Christians.

See also in **Matthew 18:12** KJV: *How think ye? if a man have an hundred sheep, and one of them be gone astray, doth he not leave the ninety and nine, and goeth into the mountains, and seeketh that which is gone astray?*

Logion 108

Jesus said, "He who will drink from my mouth will become like me. I myself shall become he, and the things that are hidden will be revealed to him."

Interpretation:

Out of his **mouth** came a two edged sword, and that was Truth and Understanding. It is not enough to receive the knowledge of Truth as food for the soul, you must also receive the Spirit of Understanding to **drink** with it.

When the soul receives both it becomes a faithful witness and a Christ. This was always the mission of Jesus, to lead other sols to the Truth and Christhood.

John 14:12 KJV *Verily, verily, I say unto you, He that believeth on me, the works that I do shall he do also; and greater works than these shall he do; because I go unto my Father.*

To believe **on** Jesus is to believe on the Way, the Truth and the Life.

In **John 14:6** KJV: Jesus says; *I am the way, the truth and the life.*

Logion 109

Jesus said, "The kingdom is like a man who had a hidden treasure in his field without knowing it. And after he died, he left it to his son. The son did not know (about the treasure). He inherited the field and sold it. And the one who bought it went ploughing and found the treasure. He began to lend money at interest to whomever he wished."

Interpretation:

It is left to each soul to discover the ***treasure hidden*** within their mind, and that treasure is the Spirit of Understanding. If you do not search for it the Truth will have no value, and you will lose your inheritance which is eternal life.

You alone are the ruler of your inner domain. It is you who has complete authority. If you let others rule your mind it is as if you have ***sold*** it.

If you sell what you have within to those who have not found their own treasure, they will search and find what you have and use it to profit for themselves. You have to become your own master and protect yourself and all that you have that is good and right. To sell your domain is to sell your soul.

See also in **Matthew 13:44-46** KJV: *Again, the kingdom of heaven is like unto treasure hid in a field; the which when a man hath found, he hideth, and for joy thereof goeth and selleth all that he hath, and buyeth that field.*

Logion 110

Jesus said, "Whoever finds the world and becomes rich, let him renounce the world."

Interpretation:

The world in which we exist is the mind, and it is in the mind that we search for and find knowledge. The most precious of all knowledge is knowledge of the Self. When this is found the search for knowledge is over and the mind becomes irrelevant for a time and so is ***renounced*** as all of the Self's focus of attention is fixed upon the Self.

Knowledge is spiritual treasure, and the most precious treasure is Truth; it is Truth that makes us ***rich*** and sets us free when understood.

Logion 111

Jesus said, "The heavens and the earth will be rolled up in your presence. And the one who lives from the living one will not see death." Does not Jesus say, "Whoever finds himself is superior to the world?"

Interpretation:

This logion speaks of the moment that full enlightenment occurs. It is as if the Self has returned to its first awakening in the beginning when it said let there be light. The end is the same as the beginning. The whole mine is full of light, and out of that light appears an image of the Self, and then your whole being is permeated by a love that cannot be described, and there is felt a perfect peace. There also is your perfected soul that lives from the Self's righteous desire, never again to see death that has now been banished. There are no more tears of sorrow, no more fear or guilt, no more fear of anything, and no more want for all desires are fulfilled. It is there that you come to find yourself and realize that you are *superior to the world* within, because you are its creator.

Logion 112

Jesus said, "Woe to the flesh that depends on the soul; woe to the soul that depends on the flesh."

Interpretation:

Woe to the physical body *that depends on the soul* for its animation and survival. The physical body will eventually cease to function, no matter how much the soul takes care of it.

Woe to the soul that depends on the physical body for its life because that soul is already experiencing death, and it too will become a corpse.

There is no afterlife for a physical body, so how can there be an afterlife for a soul that believes itself to be a physical body?

This is why Jesus said in **Matthew 8:22** KJV; *let the dead bury the dead.*

Logion 113

His disciples said to him, "When will the kingdom come?" <Jesus said,> "It will not come by waiting for it. It will not be a matter of saying 'here it is' or 'there it is.' Rather, the kingdom of the father is spread out upon the earth, and men do not see it."

Interpretation:

The kingdom of the father is the mind of righteous desire, it is full of Love, Truth and the Light of Understanding.

The righteous mind is already *spread out upon the* sub conscious mind, and souls *do not see it* or realize it.

The kingdom will not come by waiting for it, because it is already here.

Where is the kingdom? It is right before your eyes. The images that you are seeing now are painted on the canvas of your mind.

See also in **Luke 17:21** KJV: *Neither shall they say, Lo here! or, lo there! for, behold, the kingdom of God is within you.*

Logion 114

Simon Peter said to him, "Let Mary leave us, for women are not worthy of life." Jesus said, "I myself shall lead her in order to make her male, so that she too may become a living spirit resembling you males. For every woman who will make herself male will enter the kingdom of heaven."

Interpretation:

When **Simon Peter** spoke these words to Jesus it was because he knew that **Mary** believed herself to be a physical being with a female gender. It is those who believe themselves to be no more than a physical being that **are not worthy of life**, which means they are not worthy of spiritual understanding.

Simon Peter and the rest of Jesus' disciples were just the same when he met them, because each of them had the belief that they were no more than physical beings. The difference was that their physical body gender was **male**.

Jesus had already taught his disciples that they were not physical beings and that it was their souls that animated their physical bodies. Jesus had also taught them that every soul is spiritually **male**, and it is the mind that is referred to as being **female**.

Jesus said he would *lead* (teach) Mary *in order to make her* realize that she was a soul, and with that understanding she would *become a living spirit* like the other disciples.

Every woman who realizes that she is a spiritual being *will enter the* mind of righteous desire (the father).

Jesus never saw people as physical beings, he always saw the real person inside. The souls of everyone are all equal in nature, gender and worth. You are not your physical body that is of this world; you are a spiritual entity.

ABOUT THE AUTHOR

My Journey to Enlightenment

My life did not begin in this world, I have always known that and because of this, there have been times when I felt that I had an unfair advantage in life. My earliest memories have always remained vivid and I know for sure that my life has always been protected, though not from suffering or from the cold hearts of natural man. Looking back I have experienced a great deal of the things that hurt us most in life, and this has led to a profound understanding of the suffering of others. I have also experienced love and the compassion of others, and so I look back with gratitude for all of my experiences; I learnt well.

I would like to take you back now, to my earliest memory of this, my life's journey.

I stood upon the precipice that separates the spiritual realm from the material realm. It was a place so high above the world, one that can only be traversed by a soul. I turned to my left and there stood a being dressed in a long blue, loose fitting robe. The being's long hair had the appearance of a soft yellow gold that flowed below the shoulders. The face portrayed that of a long known friend and radiated peace and love beyond description and although I could discern no gender, I felt the appearance of both.

The precipice where we stood was in darkness, and was like a ledge protruding out between the two realms. In this place, I was unable to look back with either eyes or mind. It was a place where I would choose the next path on my soul's journey.

As I looked down upon the earth, I was filled with sorrow as the cries of many beat against my soul. I had found my way out of that prison and to return once more, would be for the sake of Love. It was for all of the world's imprisoned souls who are my family. As I looked into the world at the unfolding lives of many precious souls, my eyes came to rest on one whose heart was good, even though her suffering had been much, to her I would entrust my soul.

The Angel spoke in a gentle voice 'have you chosen' and I said 'I have', and I found myself leaving the realm of Love and falling alone to earth, into forgetfulness. It was there that I would strive once more, to find the Truth I had forgotten, a Truth that would be found through the Love I carried within.

This is a poem that I wrote to express my experience.

The Return

Drifting as if from some ancient time,
my conscious became aware

There was no light or dark or sound,
no sense of movement or brush of air

If there was a past the gate was sealed
and no future was in sight

It was then I crossed the barrier
to the place of dark and light

An endless stretch of sparkling jewels,
were strewn across my way

And each were made of countless stars
where souls would come to play

I drifted on through this wondrous place
as if guided by an unseen hand

Have I journeyed to this cosmic shore
to find one grain of sand?

At last I saw my journeys end
I knew this place was right

The bluest jewel and brightest pearl
bathed in brilliant light

Another barrier lay ahead
for which I had the key

Where soul and body are joined as one
and a mother waits for me
I'll lay and wait in that warm place
until my time of birth

Then with this gift I bring with me
spread love upon the earth

Continued...

For a moment nothing existed, and then I awoke in the dressing room of another reality, waiting to make my entrance on to the stage of life. I had no concept of what awaited me, and all I could see was an orange glow through the curtain and all I could hear were the sounds of a play in progress and I understood nothing. This time in the womb, was one of peace, it was the calm before the storm.

I recall those days before birth so vividly, almost as if it were yesterday. I remember knowing that I was to be born, that I would be leaving that place, but of what waited outside, I knew not. How frightening it was to leave that place. The first thing I experienced was fear, but I soon found myself being comforted in the warm and protecting arms of the one I had chosen. It was then for the first time, that I felt the powerful and beautiful bond of love flowing through every part of my being. I was here and for the moment, I was safe. I remember how strange the world seemed in those first weeks. I would look around and although I could see clearly, I couldn't understand what I was seeing, voices were the same, it was all a foreign language to me.

We all come into the world as innocent children, bathed in forgetfulness. We begin our journey with only the love we have brought to defend us from the indoctrinations of those already here. So there I was, born in 1948, content in my charity given clothes, a happy and cheeky free spirited child, not knowing the things of the world, a soul whose mind would become another battleground for light and darkness.

All through my life I've had strange experiences. Even as a child I had a reoccurring dream of a sea that was so calm and still that it looked like glass. It gave the feeling of perfect peace and tranquility which I felt through my whole body. The problem was that it would then turn all spiky, causing a terrible feeling and then an old galleon ship would go sailing by. In those years, I seemed to have developed a natural ability to go deeply into thought, where my focus was complete, clear and undisturbed. For the duration of my meditation, neither the world nor my body seemed to exist. All of my time spent in meditation was given to questioning and even as a child, those questions were mainly concerned with who I was, where I was and why I was here.

I left school at the age of 15 and had no further formal education. By the age of 17 I had already considered and dismissed many ideas. I've always been extremely self-aware that my consciousness was of a different nature to my physical body, and I guess this is what drove me with such a passion to find answers, but it was not that alone. You see, I have had many psychic experiences, some of which have shaken my reasoning and logic to the core. I have always tried to keep an open mind, preferring to look for logical answers, but of all the books that I read, nothing seemed to satisfy my questioning, in fact a lot of them seemed to come from the realms of fantasy. To search for the truth can be very frustrating. Out of all the books that ever I read, only one phrase stuck in my mind sometimes you have to give in to win'.

I didn't realize the profound significance of this, even in the years that followed.

I was christened in church as a child, and I later went to Sunday school for religious teaching and to church on the odd occasion later in life. I searched there for the truth also, but I always saw Jesus as someone greater than the father God they told me about, and I saw the church's teachings were in conflict with the teachings of Jesus and love.

So I put Christianity aside and continued on my spiritual quest. It was a quest that seemed impossible and my enthusiasm for it began to fade. I was not prepared to live by blind faith or fantasy. Everything was coming to a breaking point.

I was now in my 50s and my 30 year marriage was coming to an end. I looked back over my life and it was strewn with one suffering after another. I had always been loving, caring, compassionate and forgiving, that is except for the few times I rebelled, yes I made 'mistakes', but I always suffered deep inside for them. I thought about the world and the cruelty and injustice of it all. It was then that I realized that something had been planted deep in my psyche as a child, a God who created everything, an angry vengeful, jealous and vain God whose purpose for creation was for us to worship and obey him and if you didn't meet the standards required, the suffering felt on earth was nothing compared to what was waiting.

The belief in this God had been hiding deep inside me and was now surfacing. So now we had a culprit, one who stood against everything that I believed was good and right, against love itself and in my mind, I ranted and raved at him.

All I wanted was to stand before this God and have my say, come eternal hell and damnation, it didn't matter. I would stand against any God who stood against love.

A couple of years later, when I was free and living on my own, I decided to make the best of myself that I could. I actually lost 2 stone (12.7k) in just two weeks. I felt great! Then as fate would have it, I caught the most horrendous chest infection. My breathing was barely discernable and I had a heart attack. I was being worked on at the hospital when my heart just gave in and stopped. I woke up with burn marks on my chest. I was covered in bruises and on a machine administering antibiotics. Seems God didn't want to see me then either. It was about a year later than my life would change forever.

My Pre-enlightenment State

There came a point in my life, when through forgiveness, I had found a measure of peace and in a quiet moment, my mind once again fell on my quest for answers. I had suffered so much, but then so had others, and it was usually at the hands of the unloving, who always seem to be greatly rewarded for their actions. It was time to look at myself and my life with complete honesty. I reasoned that it would not profit me if I didn't face myself and my beliefs with unbiased logic and reasoning.

My first question was 'is there life after death?' My pre-birth memories were anchored so far in the past that for the first time, I began to doubt them and I had no memory of knowledge relating to life after this one. So I faced death and I was left with the only two possibilities; either death was an end to awareness, in which case I wouldn't even know that I had died. I just would not exist anymore, or life continues. I wasn't sure either way, but an end to awareness sounded the best option, but what then of my loving nature? Was it all for nothing? Was it no more than a mental condition that had robbed me of enjoying this one finite life?

I reasoned that it didn't matter. What mattered was that I had made the lives of others better. I had contributed to a better world. I knew that it was the way to be. It was good and right. My life had not been wasted and I and countless others would not have suffered so much if there had been more love in the world.

I decided to remain true to my loving nature and carry on living my life the way that I had always done, regardless of what came.

Next I looked at all of the knowledge that I had gained throughout my life, and I realized that I knew nothing of worth, nothing except that love is the way. Possessions are worthless, people are priceless and the greatest delusion is that we need more than love.

So there I was, emptied of desire, I did not even need my love fulfilled, to give was enough for that is where my pleasure lay.

In this knowledge I found a peace that I had never known in this life. I was free of emotional baggage. I had done my best in this life, and given the world that I was born into, I reasoned that I had done well, I had not been overcome and my love remained undefeated against all the odds. For this, I gave myself credit, and I stepped forward, happy with who I was; I had stepped out of the game of life.

We come with the knowledge of what is right and wrong (good and evil), but knowledge alone is worthless unless acted upon, and you cannot act upon the knowledge of what is good and right with sincerity, unless you first acknowledge its truth.

For three weeks, I was happier than I ever was. I was free, no more searching and no more questions. My cup was empty and desires silenced.

My Enlightenment Experience

My three weeks of pleasurable existence had just come to the end. Enlightenment was the last thing I would have thought about, and was no more than a word that I had encountered, somewhere in the pages of the books I had read in the distant past. My thoughts were not even on anything spiritual. It was then that the completely unexpected happened.

I found myself disembodied in a place full of light and I was not afraid. The first thing that I realized was that I alone occupied the space that I was in, as an aware entity.

I felt my existence as an individual entity and I knew that I was immortal and indestructible.

Images appeared in front of me at a short distance, they were images of people in the world, lost in forgetfulness, striving for material things and causing all manner of hurt to each other in their pursuit. The madness of the world was unfolding before me. I felt like shouting out to them, to wake them from their blindness, but no words came. I didn't feel their suffering at that time as much as I normally would, but I felt their longing for Truth.

It was then that I felt a presence and I knew that it was my own. Still I felt no fear; it all seemed so natural. I have no words to do justice for what happened next. I felt what I can only describe as pure love wash through every part of my being, and it was as if my eyes were fully opened, and I felt my consciousness expand. I realized that there are things that the normal consciousness is incapable of perceiving or understanding.

I looked at the images of the world once more, and I decided that I would do what I could to help, for what I then realized, was all of my family. I was then back in the world once more, changed forever. Although Christianity lay some distance in my past, the first things that sprang into my mind were 'what have they done? He died for nothing' and I will not hide the fact that it was of the church and Jesus that I was thinking.

Those who saw me after my experience would stare at me unable to understand what they were seeing. All they could say is that I was glowing somehow, but they had no words to describe it. I felt it too. It was perfect peace, confidence and love.

I didn't ask for enlightenment, I didn't ask for anything. I put myself last, and love for others first, but we already knew that it was the way, even though some have tried to take us another way.

Expanded Consciousness

Enlightenment results in a massive expansion of consciousness and through that expansion, comes the ability to receive incredible amounts of knowledge in a moment of time, as one concept that is fully understood. The difficult part is then passing on that knowledge to others in a way that they can understand. Being a person of limited and basic education, means that my communication and grammar skills have caused me some difficulty in respect of passing on what I have learnt. It has been a struggle but it's getting easier.

When consciousness is expanded through enlightenment, it is as if everything is realized in one concept, it is a knowing, like a full and sudden awakening.

Imagine that somewhere in your memories, there is a large store of knowledge sealed like a great library, knowledge that you once knew but had forgotten about. Now imagine that door being flung open, and you suddenly realize and remember all that you had known. With that knowledge you then look at your life journey, and in your embarrassment you say 'I didn't know, I didn't realize'. Then you look at others in the world who are still in forgetfulness, and you look with righteous judgement and with compassion.

You know in your heart that some will accept what you reveal, and find comfort. You also know that many will reject what you say and even hate you for your teachings, because in their forgetfulness, they prefer to live without guilt and compassion, preferring the pleasures of the world and self-gratification, even at the expense of the suffering to others, whose pain and hardship they choose to ignore, unless it affects their reputation in the community and threatens to reveal their true nature and beliefs.

Who are the deluded, but those who think that they need only the things of this world.

There is an awakening occurring in the world today, on a scale never before seen. It is the birth of the expanding consciousness, and it is found in those who acknowledge what is good and right, it is found in those with Love and a desire for Truth, those with empathy and spiritual understanding.

It is to these that I first offer my service, for they are capable of accepting and understanding divine knowledge. They are ready for their Spiritual Evolution, they are almost ready, to stand in the Light and know themselves.

Love and Blessings,

William

The authors other published books:

Gospel of Mary Magdalene Fully Interpreted

Genesis the Beginning – The Secret Teachings, The first 96 verses Fully Interpreted

The Loving Souls Survival Guide

Williams email: ltmol@hotmail.co.uk

Williams website: https://www.lovethemeaningoflife.com

Made in United States
Orlando, FL
24 December 2023

41649513R00124